The Story of
THERESE NEUMANN

Gott befohlen!

Schwester Neumann.

THE STORY OF
Therese Neumann

By

ALBERT PAUL SCHIMBERG

THE BRUCE PUBLISHING COMPANY
MILWAUKEE

Nihil obstat: JOHN A. SCHULIEN, S.T.D., Censor librorum
Imprimatur: ✠ MOYSES E. KILEY, Archiepiscopus Milwaukiensis
22 Julii, 1947

In obedience to the decree of Pope Urban VIII and in conformity with
the Apostolic Constitution *Officiorum ac munera* of Pope Leo XIII, I
declare that I claim no more than a purely human consideration for the
extraordinary gifts of grace reported in this book, and that I thereby
submit at all times and unreservedly to the judgment of the Catholic
Church.

THE AUTHOR

To

My Sisters

and Nieces

Author's Note

INTEREST in the Konnersreuth case began for the author in 1928, when the late Rev. Joseph Reiner, S.J., of Marquette and Loyola Universities, gave him a small German book on Therese Neumann and suggested that it be translated into English.

The translating of this book led to an exchange of letters with the author, Friedrich Ritter von Lama, and to the translating of two more of his books on the Bavarian stigmatist. It led also to the reading of Dr. Fritz Gerlich's two-volume examination of the Konnersreuth phenomena and considerable other material, making it possible to keep in touch with the subject until the rise of Hitlerism. Not long after he had written of Dr. Gerlich's death at the hands of the Nazis, letters ceased to come from Ritter von Lama, and later it was learned that he had shared Dr. Gerlich's fate.

For some years before the outbreak of World War II, the author had no authentic word concerning Konnersreuth and, of course, none came during the conflict. An exception was the book, *Mystical Phenomena in the Life of Theresa Neumann,* by Archbishop Teodorowicz, of Lemberg, which was published in this country and

England in 1940. After the defeat of Germany, it was learned that Therese Neumann was alive, and the visits of American soldiers to her village revealed that the phenomena had not ceased. There was a renewal of interest on the part of those already acquainted with the case, and many hitherto unacquainted with it began to be interested. It was suggested that a new book would be opportune, to tell what had happened during and after the long silence and to retell the story from its beginning for those who knew nothing of the stigmatist's life.

In the writing of this book the author has had generous help. He is especially indebted to the Rev. Stephen Klopfer, Dr. Max Jordan, and Erwein Freiherr von Aretin; to the Rev. A. S. Carney, Mrs. J. W. Hayes, Robert D. Bourguignon, and Lieut. Col. J. W. Hayes, Jr., for pictures; and to the editors and authors who have permitted him to use quotations from books, pamphlets, articles, and letters. He wishes also to thank all others who helped him in any way.

Contents

The Story of
THERESE NEUMANN

T HE soldiers who thronged to see Therese Neumann after V-E Day in 1945 gave her at once the high homage which valor is quick to evoke. They knew at once that she is a heroine. They saw the stigmatist of Konnersreuth and were filled with amazement and with awe. They wrote home about what they had seen and felt in her presence, and in this way many in the United States heard about one of the strangest lives of our time.

Many Americans, aware of Konnersreuth before the war, had heard nothing about Therese Neumann while the conflict lasted, and did not know what might have happened to her; if, indeed, she still lived. For them, the first word came in Max Jordan's dispatch of March 26, 1945: "COLOGNE — Theresa Neumann, stigmatized peasant woman of Konnersreuth, Bavaria, is still alive and unharmed, according to reliable information obtained here from Catholic sources."[1] Soon afterward, reports began to be received of visits to Konnersreuth by soldiers of the American occupation forces.

The G.I.'s and the soldiers of other countries who visited

[1] National Catholic Welfare Council News Service, Washington, D. C.

Therese Neumann saw one who has lived a life of heroic, voluntary suffering for more than twenty years. They learned that she endured, and continues to endure, pain as great as some of them suffered or saw their comrades suffer on battlefields or in prison camps. Their duty as soldiers had sent them into combat; she had fought on mystic battlefields out of love, love of God and her fellow men. They, looking upon her in the agony of her Passion ecstasy, could appreciate perhaps more keenly than others the full extent of her suffering. They would agree with the army doctor of World War I who wrote: "I have never seen a picture of such immeasurable pain as Therese Neumann presents. The greatest tragic actress in the world would never be able to produce anything so amazing and yet so natural." Many of the soldiers left Konnersreuth with an impression like that of this physician visitor of more than ten years ago: "With my own eyes, I have proved to myself and given myself an accounting: that the religious ecstasy of this poor girl, a fact that was ascribed to hysteria, bears the stamp of something beyond all measure, something eternal."[2]

One of the many soldiers who saw the stigmatist of Konnersreuth was Lieut. Robert Bourguignon, of Green Bay, Wisconsin. In a letter to his parents he wrote that Therese Neumann "doesn't act pious or anything like that." He described her as a "sweet person," and added: "You can see happiness in her."[3] Lieut. Bourguignon, like many other American soldiers, received from Therese a

[2] Hynek, R. W., *Konnersreuth: A Medical and Psychological Study of the Case of Teresa Neumann*, translated and adapted by L. W. Sheppard (London: Burns, Oates and Washburne, Ltd., 1932), Chap. 2, p. 52.

[3] The *Catholic Herald Citizen*, Milwaukee, Aug. 4, 1945.

holy picture with her autograph, her name written with one of the hands which, he could see plainly, bear the marks of the nails.

In a letter dated February 21, 1947, Mr. Bourguignon gives additional information on his Konnersreuth visit when he was an officer of the United States Army in Germany. "You can see love and kindness in her eyes," he writes of the stigmatist, "and while we were there she couldn't do enough for us. About five or six of us went into Father Naber's home and we shook hands with Theresa. She immediately went out and got chairs for us." She said she wished she could talk English. "We took many pictures of her, but she was sort of afraid of the camera. Theresa appeared to be a jolly sort of person, and on the plumpish side."

From Konnersreuth Mr. Bourguignon and the Americans with him went to the home of Therese Neumann's brother, Ferdinand, about 20 kilometers away. He was deaf in one ear because of a mine explosion "when trying to open a road block for the American troops." Ferdinand showed the visitors motion pictures he had taken of Therese in her Passion ecstasy and receiving Holy Communion in the village church on a feast day. On this occasion she had a vision of Christ in the Host. "Her face reflected very much joy and her arms were outstretched, trying to reach our Lord."

Mr. Bourguignon is among the visitors to Konnersreuth who mentions Therese's motherly devotion to refugee children. "She goes all around and gets what food she can for the children, the poor, and the sick. She is a sort of nurse." A physician from Innsbruck, Tyrol, tells that when he visited the stigmatist in 1944, she talked with animation about home remedies, because there were from ten to twenty people who, in the absence of doctors, came to her for simple help in minor ailments or injuries.

Pfc. Henry E. Melton, Jr., of Detroit, sent back to the United States an interesting account, representative of the soldiers' reaction to Konnersreuth. His letter from Leopolds Grün began: "Dear Family, It happened — my life's ambition — I can still hardly believe it. I saw Theresa Neumann and spoke with her in German and made friends with her and her birds. It was wonderful. I wish I had time to write for hours now, but I don't. I will write as much as I can. First, you must promise to procure a copy of the Biography of Theresa for the whole family to read, so they'll know all the details of her miracles. And then they can fit in the things I saw with the whole story. . . .

"She's a very simple, unassuming peasant woman of 46. And for the past 17 years she has eaten or drunk nothing. I asked her if she felt any hunger and she said 'No, and no thirst, either.' I saw the large red scabs on her hands, where the blood flows on Friday and during Holy Week. I didn't see the other wounds. I went with Fr. Kalenda, the chaplain from Grand Rapids, and I am really grateful to him for taking me. He spoke in Latin to the old priest, who has been in Konnersreuth since Theresa was eleven. And the priest showed us a set of white outer garments worn by Theresa on Good Friday.

"First, the headpiece has bloodstains on it in the shape of the crown of thorns. Then the blouse that was over two undergarments has bloodstains spattered all over it from her bleeding from the 'Scourging at the Pillar.' At the wrists the bleeding was very intense, from pouring out of her hand wounds when she holds her hands out-stretched during her reliving of the Passion. Then on the right shoulder of the garments is a big solid patch of blood where the cross was carried by Christ. Over her heart also is a big, wide bloodstain (all this shows on the garments). Then Father showed us a big piece of gauze she wears over her heart wound. It was completely soaked up with, now dry, blood, and in the center is a big scab that stayed on the gauze when it was removed. It shows the shape of the wound opening and it looks like a sword wound."

Pfc. Melton sent with his letter rough sketches of the bloodstained garments which he saw in Konnersreuth. "It is all very impressive," he wrote, "but Theresa looks per-fectly normal (except for the Stigmata) and she is sweet and lovable. She asked me many questions and was so excited when I told her about my birds and pets. She took us from the priest's house to her house — just Father and his driver and me, and I saw her birds and her grotto and the altar in her room. We had to get back but she didn't want us to go. She wanted to talk about birds. She gave me a real nice picture of St. Francis with his birds. He also had the Stigmata."[4]

Another G.I. who went to Konnersreuth and wrote home about it is Sgt. Thomas McAllister, of Albany, New York: "We went to Konnersreuth, about 100 miles from here, and saw Therese Neumann. As you know,

[4] *Our Sunday Visitor*, Huntington, Ind., Youth Section, Feb. 10, 1945.

she suffers the agony of the Passion of Christ on about 35 Fridays of the year. We were all thankful that yesterday was one of them. . . . Soon after we arrived in her room she turned to her right and spoke to the Good Thief. We stayed until she said 'It is consummated,' bowed her head and fell asleep. Her wounds stopped bleeding immediately. She is entirely conscious (during her agony) hearing everything that goes on. . . . The chaplain who happened to be there blessed her and she said: 'Thank you, Father. God be with you and your soldiers.' She then asked her parish priest where each of us had come from.

"I am enclosing a holy picture that is signed by Therese. She cannot write during her passion but she had several prepared, at least enough for the eight or ten of us who were allowed to enter the door of her home. The inscription on the card is: 'God bless you. Therese Neumann.' "[5]

Thus wrote the lads who had known North Africa, Anzio, the Normandy beach head, the Battle of the Bulge; and the later ones coming directly from the States. Thus they bear witness to the continuing phenomena of Konnersreuth, the marks of Christ's wounds in the hands of Therese Neumann, her sharing in the agony of His Passion, her visions, her abstinence from all food and drink. They give testimony also to her naturalness, her warmhearted friendliness, her Franciscan joyousness and simplicity. Most of all, they testify to her complete unconsciousness of being a heroine.

One of the many chaplains who accompanied groups of Yanks to Konnersreuth was the Rev. R. W. Schenk, S.J.,

[5] *The Evangelist*, Albany, N. Y., Feb. 8, 1946.

of St. Louis, Missouri, who wrote that he and a handful of men of the 79th Division were welcomed by the Rev. Joseph Naber, who is Therese's parish priest and spiritual director. A messenger was sent to her home near by: "She'll be right over and is always happy to meet Americans."

While the visitors waited, Father Naber told in German about this amazing spiritual child of his. He began to speak Latin fluently, and the chaplain translated his words for the soldiers who were astonished at what they heard, and were full of expectation. They were full of questions as well: "Do you kneel down when she enters? No, you don't. May you take pictures of her? Of course you may, all you want, but later on after we've spoken to her. You rush out for the cameras; you insert a fresh roll of films. You rush back to the house, and Teresa is seated in the parlor. You just presume that a person doesn't shake hands with stigmatists; she rises and you're introduced; you make a very awkward bow. She rushes to get you a chair (imagine!) and in a rapid flow of German tells you that she's very happy when priests visit her. You follow practically all of her conversation and the pastor helps out in Latin; you reflect that it's not the accepted practice to ask stigmatists to speak more slowly."

Father Schenk reports that Fräulein Neumann looks and acts like any other Bavarian peasant woman of her age. Her dress is long and usually colored, her shoes black and worn. A white shawl covers her head and is tied under the chin. "Every soldier in the room tries not to stare at her hands; invariably your eyes wander back to her hands, to the small (less than a half-inch square), scab-looking squares in the back of each hand. Teresa is not in the least embarrassed; she talks to you as your mother or your sister would talk to you, only faster. She tells you how happy she is to have soldiers visit Konnersreuth, that over 4000 have come to see her since the Americans came. She tells you how frightened all were when the bombs came and they thought they would all be killed."

A part of Father Schenk's report that has a special and poignant meaning tells of the stigmatist's happiness when Negro soldiers come to see her, because when she was a young girl she wished to be a missionary Sister in Africa. But God sent sickness which prevented the realization of her hope, and "this makes up for it in part, when colored soldiers come."

The chaplain and the G.I.'s would like to have asked to see the palms of Therese's hands, "but you don't request such things of a stigmatist." Then she told them she was going into the other room to get a holy picture for each soldier present, and that she would be glad to autograph the pictures. She returned and distributed the pictures to white soldiers and their colored comrades alike. She had a short message for the G.I.'s, asking them to join her in devotion to the Passion of our Lord, and she told them she would pray for each one.

Outside of Father Naber's house the boys of the 79th Division stood with her to take pictures. "Thousands of such pictures will be sent to America with the story of the peasant woman of Bavaria. One soldier asked: 'How do you spell stigmata, Father?' Others told of skeptics in their organizations who said it couldn't be and wouldn't take

the trouble to ride to Konnersreuth and see for themselves. But there is no doubt in the minds of those who
met Teresa on this sunny Sunday afternoon. One of the
unit officers asked: 'How is a person going to prove that
she hasn't eaten since 1927?' No one could prove that
but this same officer wouldn't take the trouble to go to
see the stigmata of Teresa's hands. Others frankly want
to go and see for themselves. They will all be welcome
at Konnersreuth."

The driver of the truck that brought Father Schenk and
the G.I.'s had to stay and guard the vehicle, so he had not
met the stigmatist. The chaplain took him into the house,
where Therese greeted him and extended her hand; she
chatted with him and got a holy picture for him, too. "As
you leave, Teresa extends her hand. You touch it reverently; you notice that the mark is on the palms as well."
Looking back, says this American Jesuit, "you do not have
the impression that you have spoken to a saint, because it
is not yours to determine who is and who is not a saint.
You do know that you have spoken to one who is especially
gifted by God, to one who is simple with the simplicity
of the Gospel, and that you have met in the midst of so
much suffering and destruction and sorrow and discontent
a person who is truly happy, possibly the happiest person
in the whole world."[6]

The French newspaper *La Croix* reports that 800 Americans had witnessed Therese Neumann's ecstasies on the
Good Friday of 1946, and that Father Naber had recently
received a letter from a Jew, an American military officer,
telling that since he had seen Therese in ecstasy he had

[6] *America*, Sept. 15, 1945, pp. 472, 473.

decided to study the Catholic religion and become a convert. The report quotes Dr. Meyer, "who personally conversed with Therese Neumann and M. l'abbé Naber for several hours on Easter Monday of this year [1946]," and says that at their departure "Therese gave Dr. Meyer and the two French officers who accompanied him autographed pictures and a token, 'Union of Prayer,' literally, 'united in holy prayer.' "[7]

A priest of the Archdiocese of Los Angeles, California, closes his account of the stigmatist since the end of World War II with this statement: During a visit of American soldiers to Konnersreuth, as they were about to take her picture, Therese smilingly remarked, "You boys with your cameras are as bad as the SS troops with guns, who used to poke their noses around here."[8]

It has been estimated that since the end of the war, the number of these "boys" who have flocked to Konnersreuth has been about 12,000. Dr. Max Jordan reports from Resl's village that "Father Josef Naber, the parish priest here, told me Theresa is delighted to meet all visitors from the United States. The Neumann home, which suffered severe damage toward the end of the war because of local fighting, now has been restored completely. . . . This year 3,000 people came to Konnersreuth on Good Friday to catch a glimpse of the woman who goes through the Passion in a kind of trance. . . . Among these visitors were many Americans, both civilians and members of the armed forces."[9]

[7] *La Croix,* Paris, Aug. 2, 1946, p. 3.
[8] Father Thomas, C.M.F., *The Mystery of Konnersreuth* (Los Angeles, 1945), p. 126.
[9] National Catholic Welfare Conference News Service dispatch from Konnersreuth, Apr. 21, 1947.

Up to April of this year, Therese Neumann had given more than 10,000 little holy pictures to as many American visitors, "because each one wished to have a memento of her." Another report says that the stream of American visitors has been large during the past twenty months, and refers to defective reports of Konnersreuth happenings in the American press.[10]

If Therese Neumann greets American soldiers so warmly and shows special interest in the United States, this may be due in part to the many American bishops, priests, and lay persons who visited her before the war; to the presence in this country of so many members of the race to which she had hoped to minister in Africa; and perhaps also to the fact that in one of her ecstasies she was told about an American mystic. The spiritual director of this unknown mystic in our country was the late Father Theophilus Riesinger, O.F.M.Cap., of the Capuchin Province of St. Joseph, which has its headquarters in Detroit.

It will have been noticed that Fräulein Neumann's first name has been spelled a number of ways, Therese, Theresa, Teresa. Therese is the form used by Friedrich Ritter von Lama and Dr. Fritz Gerlich, among the foremost writers on Konnersreuth. Therese and Theres have been used by the stigmatist in signing her name. At home and in the village in which she lives, as throughout that part of Germany, Therese is called Resl, a diminutive of her baptismal name in the Bavarian country dialect. It is pronounced Ray-sl.

10 From letter dated Feb. 27, 1947.

CHAPTER 2

Konnersreuth and the War

A SUMMARY of the situation in Konnersreuth from 1933 to the present is given by Erwein Freiherr von Aretin, a student of the Konnersreuth case since its beginning. Writing from Munich on January 27, 1947, he prefaces his account by saying that the course of the phenomena was not in the least impeded during the Nazi regime. The Passion visions continued to begin at 23 o'clock on Thursday (11 p.m.) and last until 13 o'clock Friday afternoon, when it is 3 p.m. in Jerusalem. The visions of Christ's suffering and death do not occur on Fridays between Easter and the Feast of Corpus Christi, nor on Fridays which are feast days. Though the visions may in these instances begin at 11 p.m. on Thursday, they end abruptly when the bell strikes midnight.

Freiherr von Aretin writes that the Good Friday ecstasies increased yearly in their intensity. On this day, but only then, the body of Therese Neumann shows to a greater degree the marks of the wounds suffered by the Saviour when He was scourged at the pillar; and an immense, bleeding wound appears on the right shoulder, the one on which the cross was carried. This wound disappears when the ecstatic vision ends. He tells us also that the visions during Lent of 1946 were more painful than those of earlier years.

The other visions during the year, which involve no cosuffering on Therese's part, have continued as before. During her vision of the fall of the angels on August 1 the stigmatist heard Hebrew, not Aramaic words. On All Saints' Day, November 1, 1934, says Von Aretin, Therese for the first time saw Dr. Fritz Gerlich in the glory of Paradise, among the martyrs. Dr. Gerlich, a friend of the Neumann family and writer on Konnersreuth, had been murdered at Dachau on June 30 of that year. After a vision of purgatory on November 2, 1934, the stigmatist voiced anew a plea for deceased bishops, for whom the faithful pray all too little, because their need for prayer is not realized. Therese saw Pope Pius XI enter into the glory of heaven and in a vision saw the proclamation of Pope Pius XII's election from a loggia of St. Peter's in Rome.

An arresting statement in Herr von Aretin's account is that the late Pope Pius XI sent his blessing to the mystic of Konnersreuth each day before he went to sleep, and that this Pontiff was not favorable to the reputed Vatican proposal that Therese Neumann be induced to undergo another medical examination. He declares that the proposal was set in motion while His Holiness was at the papal summer home at Castelgandolfo and that Pius XI was much displeased when he heard of it, saying: "Let the girl alone!" The Holy Father invited the stigmatist to Rome, for he wished to meet her. The writer does not know why Therese did not go to Rome, unless it was that the Nazis made it extremely difficult for anyone to leave Germany if it did not please them to have him go.

Regarding Pope Pius XII, Dr. von Aretin states that he spoke with him repeatedly about Konnersreuth when the present Pope was nuncio in Germany. At that time Archbishop Pacelli was of the opinion that a new medical investigation was capable of removing all doubts. Von Aretin is not sure whether Pius XII was ever in Konnersreuth. Once, in the state of exalted rest after Holy Communion, Therese stated that Pius XII would soon come to the belief that another medical examination — about which silence has fallen — would not have the convincing power which has been attributed to it. There would always be physicians who would find fault with the method of investigation and continue to demand one more examination.

Von Aretin asserts that, at first, the Nazis did not bother Resl of Konnersreuth. In 1933 she was able to go to Treves, where she attested the genuineness of the holy coat of Christ, preserved in the cathedral. "As I was then in prison, Therese Neumann sent me a rosary with a medal which she had touched to the holy coat. Five years later, when I was again in Konnersreuth, Father Naber told me to place the rosary on the hand of Therese after her Friday vision, when she was still blind and not yet fully returned to consciousness. I did this, whereupon she said: 'Many graces are attached to that. It has touched something that belonged to the Saviour. A saint gave it to you.' Later I teased her about having called herself a saint and she laughed heartily with me." Resl told him things regarding his imprisonment, including dangers to which he was exposed without being aware of them.

An SS trooper associated with Rudolph Hess went to Konnersreuth and was so intensely impressed that thereafter he made himself Therese's protector. This was possible for him because of Hess's strange attitude toward all occult things, including *Wünschelrute* — divining rods!

In March, 1938, Resl was to be arrested because, it was alleged, she had spread anti-Nazi reports. "Providence," says Von Aretin, "wished that I should be in Konnersreuth in those critical days." He hurried to the *Landrat*, the district official, and, providentially again, found what he had not known, that this official was a school comrade of his, a good man who even in 1938 was not afraid to have a crucifix hanging above his desk. He was glad of Dr. von Aretin's supporting intervention and the threatened arrest was prevented. When food cards were introduced at the beginning of the war, upon the writer's earnest advice Therese did not apply for any. If she had done' so, this would certainly have been exploited against the fact of her complete abstinence from nourishment. The *Landrat* gave her, instead of the allotment of food, cards for soap, which she needed very much, because on Fridays her hair is matted with blood from the crown-of-thorns wounds and the cleansing is a wearying as well as painful task.

When Hitler's troops marched into the Sudetenland in the autumn of 1938, continues this account, the border village of Konnersreuth was full of German soldiers. To protect Therese Neumann, the commanding general rode in full uniform to her home to make a call upon her and testify to his reverent respect. He was a "good Catholic Bavarian" who later became a *Feldmarschall*. Resl gave him a rosary. The troops were largely Westphalian Catholics, who flocked to the Neumann home and received rosaries from her. At one time during the war a number of French prisoners visited Therese, and because of this her father was punished with two or three months' imprisonment for having taken the Frenchmen into his home.

Freiherr von Aretin states that, contrary to rumors, the sufferer of Konnersreuth did not make any political predictions. He knows this positively. Nevertheless, he is prepared to testify under oath to two prophecies of another kind, which concerned him. On Sunday, July 24, 1938, Fürst Erich zu Waldburg-Zeil came by automobile to Hohenstein near Rottweil in Württemberg, and called on Von Aretin. He was accompanied by his brother-in-law, Archduke Theodor Salvator of Austria, and the purpose of his visit was to tell Freiherr von Aretin, on Therese Neumann's behalf, that a search of his house was about to take place, and he was advised to remove anything he did not wish to have fall into the hands of the searchers. Therese had instructed the Fürst not to write to Von Aretin, but to see him. Two days after this, on Tuesday, July 26, the house search took place and despite its negative result, Herr von Aretin was arrested. He was released August 3, 1938.

On July 5, 1939, Von Aretin wrote to Therese, asking when he might see her and talk with her about something of pressing importance. Father Naber answered on

July 6 that Resl wished to tell Von Aretin that this would
not be possible until after August 15. On July 9 the
stigmatist, while attending a first solemn Mass near Eichstätt, suffered a heat prostration three times, laming her
entire right side. On August 15, during a vision of the
Blessed Virgin's assumption into heaven, the mystic was
healed suddenly, and was again able to speak, for the first
time since July 9.

According to this chronicler of the Konnersreuth case,
when the Americans neared Therese Neumann's village in
1945, the SS troops attacked the place and took it under
sharp artillery fire, despite the fact that no American was
there. The church, Therese's home, and Father Naber's
rectory were struck and there seems scarcely any doubt
that they were deliberate targets. The damage was not very
great, however. He believes the purpose was to put blame
for the damage on the Yanks, whose conduct toward the
stigmatist was always above criticism. When Von Aretin
visited Konnersreuth early in August, 1946, the damage
was in part repaired, the Nazi-dominated period of horror
had passed forever, and peace had returned to the little
village.

La Croix states that the report of Therese Neumann's
death during the third year of the war "was nothing but
an attempt at diversion on the part of Nazi propaganda."[1]
Hitler's Third Reich lost no time banning everything connected with Konnersreuth. Von Aretin wrote recently that
during the Nazi reign he saw only two notices, both false:
one that Therese was an ardent adherent of Adolph
Hitler, the other that she was dead. He said there was a

[1] *La Croix*, Paris, Aug. 2, 1946, p. 3.

story to the effect that about 1940, while she was in an ecstatic state and blind, a visitor put into the stigmatist's hand a post card bearing Hitler's picture, and that with a gesture of abhorence the sightless woman cast the card from her and exclaimed: *"Rauch und Feuer von Hölle!"* . . . "Smoke and fire of hell!" Von Aretin reported that the ban had this good effect, it reduced sharply the number of visitors and so moderated the bother they caused Therese and her parents.[2]

The American Jesuit chaplain whom we have quoted wrote that he and all the soldiers with him had come by a roundabout way to Konnersreuth, by way of England, France, the Netherlands, and through many smashed German cities. When they reached Therese's village they found that, as is usual over there, the church was in the center of the square, "and you're amazed to see that Konnersreuth had been bombed. Some of the damage has been repaired, some of it looks like the result of shelling but you find out later that it has been bombs. Thousands of such villages had been by-passed by the war but not Konnersreuth. The church and school had escaped damage; the pastor's house across the street had not been so fortunate; his kitchen barely remained and the back yard is filled with rubble. The words of the Little Flower spoken to this German Teresa in 1939 flash through your mind. 'Do your duty and don't be concerned with what may happen.' "[3]

Another American chaplain describes his visit to Konnersreuth on September 28, 1945: "The village itself is unpretentious, not unlike hundreds of such villages, little

[2] *Berliner Hefte*, Sept., 1946, p. 256.
[3] *America*, Sept. 15, 1945, pp. 472, 473.

cow towns scattered throughout Bavaria. It is so small it did not appear on the military map we carried. A single weather-beaten sign on the main highway north of Regensburg points down a narrow dirt road to Konnersreuth. The saints have never been noted for calling attention to themselves, so no publicity agent greeted us at the crossroads, and nobody was there to say, 'This way to the home of Theresa Neumann!'

"Entering the village we found that it was badly damaged. Later we were told that since it was a Nazi stronghold the American army, as it approached, had dropped ten shells into the village, and after the Americans had captured it, the Nazis had shelled it from five different directions."

In conversation with Herr and Frau Neumann, the army chaplain learned that four of their sons had served in the army and were now at home; that the Nazis had "treated the family, and especially Theresa, with great harshness — that, before the American troops arrived, they had actually tried to kill her. She had escaped by hiding in the barn." There was the story of the local schoolmaster, a Hitlerite, "who tore the crucifix off the wall of the village school and threw it into the street, and how, instantly, the hand which performed this deed had withered and hung lifeless like a piece of rope."

Several hundred American soldiers were in Konnersreuth on the day of his visit in September, 1945, and, says the chaplain, "very reverent they were, which is unusual in soldiers." He and the priest with him were beckoned into the stigmatist's room by Father Naber. "As we reverently entered, a peculiar and indefinable odor was faintly discernible, which instantly called to mind the 'odor of sanctity' we read about in the lives of the saints. There, on the bed in this small room was Theresa Neumann. What followed was an experience I shall never forget."[4]

Additional glimpses into Konnersreuth during and after the war are given by an American officer and an Austrian priest. The officer, Lt. Col. Frank W. Hayes, Jr., of San Diego, California, was decorated many times by his own and the French governments. The Austrian priest, Father Franz Ferkala, tells about his visit to Konnersreuth in January, 1946.

Lt. Col. Hayes wrote to his mother that he and those with him reached Konnersreuth on a Thursday evening at about 8 o'clock. When they had entered Father Naber's home Therese "came out of the kitchen. I had no idea who she was until I noticed the wounds on her hands. I believe that my first thought when I had identified her was to compare her with a description of Bernadette by Franz Werfel." The stigmatist "is a short woman, just a little on the stout side, and at the time was dressed in a full black gown with white collar and a white shawl over her head. She looks much younger than her 47 years. Her skin is very soft and smooth, her eyes large and clear, and all that evening she was constantly smiling and laughing."

While this officer was present, Resl mentioned the fact that the wounds of her feet gave her some trouble in walking, and she was thinking of getting a pony. She said jokingly that as she had never ridden horseback, she wanted either two horses and a buggy or, that, what she

4 Linehan, James M., O.F.M., *A Living Crucifix* (Paterson, N. J.: St. Anthony Guild, 1946), pp. 3-7.

really wanted was an American jeep! Father Naber told
the visitors that Therese "visits the sick constantly and that
the wounds in her feet cause her a great deal of pain,"
reports Lt. Col. Hayes, and adds: "Something I didn't
know was that the SS had tried to kill Theresa several
times but had been thwarted by the townspeople."[5]

When the Americans had taken the town, two guards
were assigned to the stigmatist, much to her amusement.
She seemed not to realize at all the possibility of danger
to herself, or care about it. Neither did she make much
ado about the dangerous position in which she was placed
when she innocently picked up a metallic object in a
street of the village. It was a land mine.

Father Ferkala, who had been imprisoned at Dachau
during the war, writes of Therese Neumann's extensive
charity work. She visits the sick and helps them, and helps
the many refugees who come to Konnersreuth and vicinity
from Czechoslovakia, sent away with nothing but the
clothes on their backs. She distributes the food given by
the farmers of the district, and clothing, too, and manages
to get some tobacco for the men. "The refugees extol
Therese's eagerness to help them."

This Austrian priest stresses the fact that neither
Resl nor any of her relatives wish for publicity, or
to be pointed out. Permission to take pictures of the
stigmatist was seldom given, until the Americans sought
to photograph her again and again. When she asked Father
Naber about the matter he told her to gratify them since
it was unimportant. (*Na, machst ihnen halt die Freude,
und stellst dich hin. Ist ja nichts dabei!*) Thereupon she

[5] *The Southern Cross*, San Diego, Calif., Friday, Mar. 1, 1946.

allowed herself to be photographed innumerable times, a sacrifice though it was.

It is not true, writes Father Ferkala, that Therese vanished from the auto of the Gestapo when they attempted to arrest her. It is also untrue that she has made many prophecies. Father Naber told Father Ferkala that once Resl had an hour-long talk with a fallen-away American priest, through an interpreter, and pleaded with him to return to his priestly work, and afterward she said that he would do this and would yet do much for the welfare of souls.[6]

Writing of the war's effect on Therese Neumann's village, an American priest says: "Most of Konnersreuth's houses are gutted and burned, and even Theresa's home and the beautiful parish church were damaged, however not beyond repair. Her own room was badly damaged. The stigmatist was saved almost miraculously from injury and death. On May 3rd [1945] our American soldiers entered the village of Konnersreuth, and a few days later Saint Theresa of the Child Jesus appeared to Miss Neumann and said to her: 'Be calm and have courage, for you have been given wonderful help and a satanic plan has been counteracted by Divine Power. You knew it beforehand and had seen the terrible danger that threatened you, but Our Lord accepted your sacrifice, which was not in vain. Your mission is not ended. You must be a living and providential witness to the supernatural realities.' "[7]

This priest, Father Thomas, had visited Konnersreuth for the first time in 1928, seeking Therese's prayers for his

[6] *KIPA,* Feb. 8, 1947, Nos. 99, 100.
[7] Thomas, Fr., C.M.F., *The Mystery of Konnersreuth* (Los Angeles, 1945), p. 126.

father, who was critically ill but whose condition improved thereafter. He made a number of subsequent visits to the stigmatist's village, and regarding the present he asserts that Therese Neumann is in good health, despite the fact that she has not slept for eighteen years and continues to abstain from food and drink, Holy Communion being her only sustenance. She continues, too, to have the mystical gifts of ecstasy and visions and to suffer with Christ when she sees Him in His bitter Passion. She helps in the household tasks of her home, visits the sick and the dying, cleans the church and arranges flowers on the altars.

The Rev. George W. McHugh of Cambridge, Massachusetts, is another chaplain who visited Konnersreuth soon after the end of the war. He declares — what had never before been made public — that when Therese Neumann received her First Holy Communion, "she beheld not the consecrated Host, but Christ Himself. She did not speak of this at the time because she thought that everyone else in receiving Communion beheld Christ also." He says that when Therese receives Communion each day it is the same, she sees Christ Himself. This new fact concerning the mystic's First Holy Communion is mentioned also by Father Guy Moews, O.F.M., in his booklet, *Soldiers Saw Resl.*[8]

Father McHugh had heard that the stigmatist could tell a priest if one touched her hand. During one of his visits to the Neumann home, Father Naber told him to touch Therese's hand while she was in an ecstatic state and her eyes blinded by the flow of blood. He did so and at once the mystic said, "This is the consecrated hand

[8] Cincinnati: St. Francis Book Shop, 1947, p. 16.

of a priest who has come from over the ocean, and with whom I have spoken much." The chaplain told an American doctor who was present, a non-Catholic, to touch Therese's hand. When he did so, the stigmatist said the hand was that of one who helped the sick and who came from over the ocean.

Regarding Konnersreuth during the war, Father Mc-Hugh states that Therese is very emphatic in saying the damage to the village was done by the SS and not by the Americans. He writes that during the SS shelling Therese was with fourteen children in the cellar of a house which was hit, and it was necessary after the attack to more or less drag Resl and the children from the ruins, but none of them was hurt.

In closing his account of visits to Konnersreuth Father McHugh comments on Therese's "great affection for her donkey." He has wondered, he says, "if the foundation for such affection isn't based on the fact that this humble beast was privileged to carry the Incarnate Son of God."[9]

An account of what befell Therese Neumann and her village during World War II and at its close is contained in the *Kirchenblatt* of the deanery of Wiesbaden, Germany. The stigmatist was subjected to a house search by the Gestapo and then to a strict watch by the police. But the climax of her persecution came during the final days of the war.

"It was as though Satan wished to deliver one final heavy blow against her, and thus make her powerless at last. An SS Panzer group was stationed in the village, and

[9] From multigraphed letter dated Jan. 30, 1945.

Therese almost became the victim of its devilish attack. In the evening of April 20 (1945), just as these soldiers were about to leave the village, an SS sergeant came into the Neumann house and in the most brutal manner demanded the surrender of Therese. He threatened those present with his pistol (Therese happened to be absent) and a shooting affair [*Schiesserei*] almost occurred in the house, as she told me. Only the energetic interference of a staff doctor caused the commanding sergeant to leave the house. But this was done amid the most dire threats to level Konnersreuth to the earth. 'If you do not surrender her, we shall set fire to your hut over your heads. Then she will certainly crawl out of the building' were his words, as a witness told me."

That night the fire of the German tanks was turned upon Konnersreuth destroying seventeen houses and twenty-eight barns. "And there was not a single American soldier in the village!" (*Dabei war nicht ein einziger amerikanischer Soldat im Dorfe!*)

Meanwhile, the American Infantry near Arzberg, with only three tank destroyers, had been awaiting reinforcements. Not until they believed themselves fired upon from Konnersreuth did they send a number of shots in the direction of the village, which had already begun to burn. They did this only because they were forced to, as an American officer explained at once and apologetically at Father Naber's house. The officer showed a map, with Konnersreuth marked in red. The Yanks were commanded most strictly to spare the village as much as possible.

During the bombardment by the SS tanks, Therese

was in the cellar of the pastor's barn, which soon went up in flames, and at the same time the priest's home and the church were struck. A few minutes before the barn collapsed Therese fled from the cellar, narrowly escaping death from suffocation.

That there was actually a fiendish and determined intention to take the life of the stigmatist is proved by the words of the sergeant who had made the threat in her home and who immediately thereafter was heard to say, mockingly: "Now she is gone! Didn't I tell you?" Later five grenades were hurled against the Neumann home and tore a hole in the gable wall. Therese's father and one of her brothers were almost struck.

The writer, who tells us this, describes his visit to Konnersreuth in the week after Easter, 1946. Father Naber's house showed the effects of grenades. The priest's bedroom and the kitchen had been badly damaged. The visitor saw no one as he walked through the ruins of the barn, until at some distance he espied a woman working in the garden. A woman in a white headdress was spading energetically, and when she suddenly raised up her head and looked at him, he saw that it was Therese Neumann. "A stigmatist doing such hard physical work? And her hands, on which one saw plainly the square-shaped stigmata, gripping the spade firmly? I scarcely believed what I saw, but at once she called me by my name and, interrupting her work, seemed pleased at my coming. We were soon in a lively conversation about the events of the past few years."[10]

This visitor, who had known Therese for fifteen years,

10 *Katholisches Kirchenblatt*, Wiesbaden, July 14, 1946.

was deeply impressed by the stigmatist's healthy appearance and her joyous spirit. He had never before seen her so merry, so warmheartedly friendly, and there was about her a composure which is not common among people in these days. The child of nature, working in the garden, seemed to be united most intimately with nature and the landscape. She had become more stately, despite the war, her face fresh and full, and her eyes bright with a quiet joy. Past were the ordeals of former years and the terrible experiences of wartime. Never before had Therese been so natural and so artless.

In closing his account, this writer says that the protection of Resl and Konnersreuth was made manifest by the vision granted the stigmatist on April 29, 1945, anniversary of the beatification of St. Thérèse of Lisieux. As on earlier occasions, the Little Flower showed herself in a flood of light and told Therese to be at ease and have confidence, for the diabolical plot was frustrated and her sacrifice was acceptable to the Lord. He declares it is evident that Therese had offered herself as a sacrifice in a special manner, to save Konnersreuth and its people.

THE first intense interest of the soldiers at Konnersreuth was centered in the hands of Therese Neumann, as the interest of all visitors before and since has been centered in the hands that bear the marks of wounds which are the constantly visible proofs that Therese is a stigmatist.

Many of the visitors knew something at least about stigmatization, may have read of Anna Catherine Emmerich, perhaps of Louise Lateau; and had learned in religion classes that St. Francis of Assisi is generally held to be the first stigmatist in the history of the Church. However, the Apostle St. Paul described himself as one crucified with Christ and closed his letter to the Galatians with the statement that he bore the marks of the Lord Jesus on his body. Once, while in ecstasy, Resl in answer to a question said that St. Paul was the first stigmatist, but later, in the normal state, she unhesitatingly said that St. Francis of Assisi was the first to be stigmatized, and knew nothing of her earlier statement about St. Paul. In this instance ecstatic and natural knowledge did not agree, the natural following the traditional acceptance, the ecstatic that of the Scriptures.

The visitors to Konnersreuth knew that there had been stigmatists in the past and in faraway places. Therese Neumann is a stigmatist in the present, and for the soldiers Konnersreuth was within reach. Is it any wonder that they rode by the hundreds to the hill town, in jeeps and trucks, as people from all over the world had come in automobiles and buses before the war? Is it any wonder that every soldier and every chaplain tried not to stare at her hands, but stared? That "invariably your eyes wander back to her hands"?

While they stared at Therese's hands, the soldiers thought, as most visitors have thought, of what they had heard or read about her wound marks, recalled that she bears not only the stigmata they could see, but others, too. Her feet are wounded in the same manner as her hands. In her side there is a wound which one of her soldier-visitors described as looking like a sword wound, to judge from the bloody mark it left on the garment he was permitted to see. Her shoulders bear the marks of the scourging and of the heavy pressure of the cross, and her head has wounds like those made by a crown of thorns.

The G.I.'s and their chaplains knew, or were told by Father Naber, that Therese's stigmata bleed during her ecstasies of the Sacred Passion, when she sees and shares in the agony of Him whose body was bruised for us more than 1900 years ago. Her eyes, too, bleed during the Passion ordeal. They were told how the first stigma appeared on the body of Fräulein Neumann, then others; what men said when this was bruited about, and what Resl has to say about her stigmata.

This is the way in which the first stigma was bestowed:

On February 13, the Saturday before Shrove Tuesday in 1926, Therese became so ill while at Mass that she had to leave the village church. When she reached her home she had to go to bed at once, and the attending physician diagnosed the sickness as la grippe or influenza. To this was added a very painful ear trouble which recurred after a lapse of two years.

On Thursday night, March 4, 1926, Resl was again lying on the sickbed to which she had been chained in former years by a succession of illnesses which had, however, yielded to a succession of astonishing cures. She was very weak and the pain was so intense that she could scarcely pray, not even the Way of the Cross. This condition continued, so that the ensuing Holy Week she could not properly understand that the period of special devotion to the Passion of our Lord had begun.

As she lay thus on her bed of suffering, Therese suddenly saw the Divine Redeemer in the Garden of Gethsemani. "I saw Him kneeling on the ground, and I saw everything else in the garden, the trees, the rocks, and also the three disciples. They were not sleeping, but in a sitting position, leaning on a rock. They looked quite exhausted. All at once I felt such vehement pain in my side that I thought my last moment had come. Then I felt something running down my body. It was blood."[1] The blood kept on trickling until toward noon of the next day, and Resl remained so weak that she hardly knew where she was or what she was about.

A week later, March 11, she did not know it was

[1] Pacificus, Father, O.M.Cap., *The Story of Teresa Neumann* (London and Dublin: Burns, Oates and Washburne, Ltd., 1945), p. 15.

Thursday. During that night she saw the Saviour first in the Garden of Olives and then at the pillar of scourging, and the wound in her side bled again. During the night of March 18 she saw Christ in Gethsemani and as He was crowned with thorns, and the side wound bled once more. On Passion Friday (the Friday before Holy Week) she saw the Saviour carrying the wood of the cross and falling under its weight. The wound in her side bled again at this time and an open wound appeared on the back of the sufferer's left hand. Her mother noticed it and asked what had happened, and Resl answered that the wound had come of itself. It was March 26, 1926, and Therese Neumann was two weeks from her twenty-eighth birthday.

Therese has said: "My parents were as yet unaware of what had happened to me. It was possible for me to hide the side wound from them until Maundy Thursday. I did not yet have the other wounds. My most loyal confederate was my sister Zenzl. I could depend upon her completely, she would say nothing. To her I said now, 'You know Mother has such a fear whenever anything happens. Wash it all away, without letting Mother see.' My sister did as I wished, quietly, without bothering me with many questions."

Resl wore a large black cloth over her shoulders so that the bloodstains were less noticeable. Her parents, she said, thought it was because of her cold. One day her mother told her she ought not to wear the same black cloth every day. "You lie there like an old grandmother." She took the cloth away, but Therese asked for it so insistently that it was given back to her the next day. On Holy Thursday Therese's father discovered her secret. Resl had another

vision of Christ in Gethsemani, and that evening her side
bled. Herr Neumann was in the room and saw how Resl
drew forth a cloth. She asked him for another cloth, and
when he offered her one she asked for a larger piece. He
noticed how she folded it eight times and then slyly
attempted to hide it under the cover. Therese explains:
"But in my weakness I was somewhat awkward and so
he noticed it anyhow, and my long and carefully concealed
secret was uncovered. Father found the blood-drenched
cloth and showed it to Mother. In this way my parents
became aware on Holy Thursday of the strange flow of
blood from my side, though they had not seen the wound
and did not know its connection with the bleeding."

On Good Friday, continues the stigmatist's account,
during her vision of the Agony in the Garden and while
she was unconscious of her surroundings, the blood flowed
from her side in such quantities that the cloth padding
could no longer absorb it and it penetrated even through
her night jacket. "Besides, everyone could see the blood
which now flowed from my eyes so copiously that it covered my whole face. Now my parents began to realize
what had happened to me, and they could scarcely believe
their eyes. Nor did they know anything as yet about the
wounds in my hands and feet. For these wounds had
appeared also on Good Friday for the first time. Exactly
when I received them I myself do not know. On Good
Friday they were simply there.

"Before that I did not know at all that I would have
these wounds. Neither did I have any idea of them during
the vision. I could not think of myself at all, did nothing
but look at the Saviour. When I came to once more after

the vision on Good Friday, I felt that blood was running down from my hands and feet, too. I could not, however, see what it was, because I could not open my eyes, on account of the blood. Not until in the evening did I say to my sister: 'Zenzl, see what is the matter with my hands and feet that they hurt me so!' My sister bandaged the wounds, without letting my parents know about them, so they would not be needlessly alarmed."[2]

On Holy Saturday her parents found out what had happened to Resl's hands and feet. Because of her intense suffering on Good Friday, they had waited until the next day to rearrange their daughter in her bed. When they undertook to change the bedding they saw the stigmata of the hands and feet, and in their amazement and anxiety they notified the parish priest. He, learning from the parents what had taken place and also Therese's reluctance in the matter, told her to let him see the wounded hands and feet in obedience to him as her pastor and spiritual director.

Father Naber was so moved by what he saw that it was some time before he regained his composure. He saw that Therese Neumann bore on the back of each hand and on the instep of her feet, "round, open wounds from which clear blood flows." The wounds caused her intense pain; she said that the feeling was as if something "was sticking in there." The side wound pained her, too, and here the seat of the pain seemed deeply inward. The wound in her side is not where Christ was pierced by the lance, on the right side, but is directly over the heart.

2 Witt, Leopold, *Konnersreuth im Lichte der Religion und Wissenschaft* (Waldsassen: Albert Augerer, 1929), Vol. 1, pp. 182–185.

After the Good Friday of 1926, all of Resl's stigmata remained open wounds for fourteen days, until April 17 of that year. They did not bleed continuously but were always moist, so that they had to be bandaged. At this time she spoke of the hand wounds as being raised along the outer edges, with little depressions or hollows toward the center of each wound. Then on April 17 a change took place. A transparent membrane, like gelatine, or suggesting even glass or celophane, formed over the bright reddish flesh of the wounds, so that Resl could again wash her hands as before. This formation of a thin skinlike substance over the open wounds was so remarkable that it drew astonished comment from Dr. Otto Seidl of Waldsassen, a near-by town considerably larger than Konnersreuth. He had attended Therese years before and was called when she again became ill on the Saturday before Lent in 1926. But he was not called in this instance until after home remedies had failed to heal the wounds while they were as yet unprotected by the membrane.

Therese and her parents took it for granted and, in fact, desired very much that the wounds would respond to the usual treatment. When they failed to do so, Dr. Seidl was called. When he saw the stigmata he examined them with the utmost curiosity and care, for he had never observed anything like this in his long practice of medicine. He reported that the side wound was 3.33 centimeters, or about 1.31 inches long. Prescribing a salve, he gave exact directions for its application. Since the wounds were not inflamed and showed no tendency to fester, they should have yielded to this treatment. Instead, poor Resl began to suffer excruciating pain, to such a degree that Father

Naber was called, and he advised removal of the bandages
which held the salve in place. Thereupon the pain ceased.
A few days later Dr. Seidl made another call and repeated
the treatment, bound the wounds, and said he himself
would remove them when he came again. Once more
intense pain set in and the wounds swelled worse than
the first time. Finally the bandages and ointment were
removed and only linen cloths placed on the stigmata.
The pain vanished then, but Therese was left with the
problem of knowing what to do. In her distress she turned
to one who had helped her in the past, St. Thérèse of
Lisieux, who had taken a prominent part in earlier happenings in their way almost as disturbing and hard to
understand as the appearance of the stigmata and the
refusal of the wounds to heal. Resl did not ask that the
wounds be taken away, nor even that they be healed,
only that she and her parents be told what to do, how
to treat them.

It was at about a quarter to three in the morning of
April 17, 1926, when the harassed Resl asked the intercession of St. Thérèse. Soon afterward, as Therese says, she
felt the linen bandages begin to loosen. She awakened
her sister Crescentia, whom everybody called Zenzl, and
asked her to turn on the electric light in the room which
they shared. The bandages were removed. Father and
mother were called and they saw that the wounds were
dry and healed without leaving scars. The wounds remained but caused Resl no pain; the reddish flesh
was visible but the wounds were as if covered by a
transparency.

Dr. Seidl, having been summoned, said to Therese and

her mother after his examination: "This is extraordinary: the wounds do not fester, they do not become inflamed. Some people declare it is a fraud, and others say it is a matter of hallucination. Neither of them speak the truth. There is not the slightest possibility of fraud." He did not prescribe any treatment, not even the exceptionally mild salve he had used, but simply bandaged the stigmata.

At this time, the wounds on the backs of Therese's hands and on her insteps were round and about the size of an American nickel, somewhat smaller than an English shilling.

Five of her stigmata have, then, been borne by Therese Neumann since the Lent of 1926. Marks of the wounds which the crown of thorns inflicted on the Saviour appeared on the stigmatist's head in November of that year. "A crown of eight wounds on the back of her head makes it necessary for the sufferer to wear a headcloth constantly." These wounds appeared after Resl had for some time experienced the pain of them without having the stigmata visible on her person. During her ecstasies of the Passion it seemed to her that thorns pierced her head and she would put up her hands in a gesture of wanting to pull them out. In like manner, when her vision was of the scourging of Jesus at the pillar, she felt the lashing of whips, especially on her back. It was only later, however, that the marks of wounds appeared on that part of her body.

The wounds of the crown of thorns appeared on November 19, 1926, but they had been bestowed on the First Friday of the month, without being known to anyone but Resl. The day on which her family became aware of these wounds was Resl's most painful day thus far in the long ordeal of stigmatization. Her suffering, as she saw the Passion of Christ, was even more intense, and her parents and others in the home wondered when she complained that the pain of the earlier Friday had remained. During the morning of November 19 blood broke through the white headdress in eight places. Her hair was clogged with blood, and when her sister tried to help her extreme care was necessary lest even a slight touch intensify the pain. Later these wounds closed, only to open and bleed in common with the other stigmata when a Passion ecstasy takes place.

Meanwhile, the side wound and those of the hands and feet underwent changes. During the first months after its appearance, the wound over Therese's heart seemed to be quite flat, then it deepened until she had the feeling that it must almost be visible through the heart and even on her back. When this stigma was bestowed, Resl said, it felt as though a sharp instrument had been plunged into her side and then withdrawn. Gradually, it seemed to her, the wound deepened, until the heart was wholly pene- trated, and this feeling was exceptionally intense on the Feast of the Sacred Heart in June, 1927.

The stigmata of the hands and feet deepened, too, until they had gone through to the palms of the hands and soles of the feet. During an ecstasy, Therese complained that someone had poured water into her palms. Upon investi- gation it was found that blood was flowing from the new openings. At the same time blood came from openings in the soles. On the backs of the hands and on the insteps these stigmata looked like blackened, encrusted spots; on the other side, however, they were somewhat smaller and rather reddish in color. Highly sensitive to the touch, they lost their hardness on Thursday evenings before Friday ecstasies and appeared more like fresh wounds.

The bloody tears which are peculiar to her case must be counted among the Konnersreuth sufferer's stigmata. She has stated that her eyes began to bleed when she suffered from an ear trouble in 1923 and 1924. But at that time the blood came seldom and only in drops, and she gave the matter little attention. Nor did her physician make any pronouncement. She never imagined that she had an eye disease, although at that time her eyes did bother her somewhat after prolonged use. Now her eyes are all right before and after the Passion ecstasies. Dr. Seidl tried without any result at all to find whence the blood came. "The doctors cannot help me and my eyes and the wounds continue to bleed, as long as it pleases God." The first profuse bleeding from the eyes took place on Good Friday, April 2, 1926, when the stigmata of the hands and feet appeared. The stigmata on the shoulder appeared on Good Friday, April 6, 1928. They disappeared thereafter, but on one occasion flowed in such quantity as to penetrate both chemise and nightdress.

A strange incident in connection with Therese Neumann's stigmatization is mentioned by a number of writers, among them Dr. Fritz Gerlich, Father Leopold Witt, and Erwein Freiherr von Aretin. On May 17, 1927, the second anniversary of St. Thérèse of Lisieux's canonization, Resl had an ecstatic vision of this saint. All at once a number of the bystanders exclaimed that the stigma of the left hand shone brightly. Father Naber, who did not see the phenomenon, had asked the Konnersreuth village teacher to take a picture of Therese. When the photographic plate was developed, there appeared on it a bright, strong light, an aura as it were, about the left-hand stigma. There is no question of a defective plate nor of any manipulation.

The soldiers and chaplains and almost all other Konnersreuth pilgrims before or since World War II saw only the stigmata of Fräulein Neumann's hands. The other wounds have been seen only by especially privileged persons and members of the Neumann family. But all of the stigmata have been described minutely, and we have been told, too, of their effect upon her who bears them. Intense pain accompanied their bestowal and in general they cause Therese suffering when they bleed during the Friday ecstasies.

For some time the stigmata of the hands prevented Therese from grasping any object firmly, and those of the feet make walking painful and difficult. Most painful of all was the side wound, particularly after it had deepened. Then it became the source of suffering to Therese each time she spoke. If she spoke with more than usual vehemence or walked fast, she had to take deep breaths and this caused a piercing pain. In time, the wounds in general ceased to hurt, excepting during the ecstasies of the Passion, and visitors see in Therese a healthy, vigorous woman, smiling and merry, giving no hint at all of what she has suffered and continues to suffer; no hint of the sustained heroism which has been hers since 1918. In that year the first of the extraordinary events took place, which had their climax in stigmatization eight years later, showered world-wide attention upon one who prefers a hidden life, and made Konnersreuth the center of a controversy which has waged for more than a quarter of a century and continues to interest an immense number of people in all parts of the world.

CHAPTER 4

The Marks of the Wounds

IN A book published in 1922,
Dr. E. Aigner declared that in his day the phenomena of
stigmatization had ceased entirely, *"dass die Erschein-
ungen des Stigmatismus heute gänzlich erloschen seien."*[1]

The Herr Doktor, a leader of Monism in Germany,
was mistaken. At least three stigmatists were living when
his book appeared. One was Sister Maria Fidelis Weiss,
who died at Reuberg in Bavaria a year after Dr. Aigner's
learned treatise was issued. Another was Anna Henle,
who lived in Aichstetten, Württemberg, and is said to
have foretold World War I. And still living is Padre Pio
of Foggio, now about 59 years of age. Like Therese Neumann in Germany, this Capuchin priest-stigmatist in
Italy has been visited by many American soldiers of the
occupation forces, some of whom have been privileged to
be present at holy Masses celebrated by him. The wounds
in his hands and feet and side became visible in September, 1918, four years before Dr. Aigner declared stigmatization a thing of the past.

When the German Monist's book appeared in 1922,

---

[1] Grabinski, Bruno, *Neuere Mystik* (Hildesheim: Franz Borkmeyer,
1924), 2 ed., p. 440.

Therese Neumann was undergoing experiences which were a prelude, which would culminate in her stigmatization four years later.

There have been known, recorded, and venerated stigmatized persons in the Church since St. Francis of Assisi received the marks of Christ's wounds on Monte Alverno in 1224, which was 702 years before Therese Neumann's first stigma appeared. Perhaps there were stigmatists, including St. Paul, before the Little Poor Man; perhaps there are bearers of the wounds in the world today of whom the world is not aware. In his book, *La Stigmatisation*, which was published in Paris in 1894, Dr. Imbert-Gourbeyre counted the stigmatists at 321, of whom 41 were men. He believed that others could be added to the list through research in the libraries and archives of Europe.

In the thirteenth century there were several stigmatists in addition to St. Francis, among them St. Lutgarde, a Cistercian, St. Margaret of Cortona, St. Gertrude, a Benedictine, St. Clare of Montefalco, an Augustinian nun. In the fourteenth century the wound bearers included the great St. Catherine of Siena, St. Lidwina of Schiedam, whose life was written by the convert aesthete, Joris-Karl Huysmans, and St. Frances of Rome. The fifteenth century had St. Catherine of Genoa, St. John of God, St. Catherine de Ricci. In the sixteenth and seventeenth centuries were Blessed Marie de l'Incarnation, a Carmelite, Blessed Carlo of Zezze, a Franciscan, and others. Among the eighteenth century stigmatists was Sister Mary Frances of the Five Wounds, a Franciscan Tertiary who died in 1791.

Among the twenty-nine stigmatists of the nineteenth century, according to Dr. Imbert-Gourbeyre's reckoning, the most widely known were Anna Catherine Emmerich, Maria von Moerl, and Louise Lateau.

Klemens Brentano, a German Romantic poet, spread wide the amazing story of Anna Catherine Emmerich, an Augustinian nun. He was devoted to her, believed whole-heartedly in the reality of her mystical gifts, and wrote an account of her visions. There has been considerable controversy regarding the reliability of Brentano's writings about this stigmatist, but little as to the genuineness of her wounds and the phenomena accompanying them.

Maria von Moerl spent her life, from 1812 to 1868, in Kaltern, Tyrol. She became an ecstatic at the age of 20 and this remained her habitual state until she died 25 years later. In addition to Joseph Görres, who wrote of her in his monumental work, *Die christliche Mystik,* those who saw her and told of their impressions included Cardinal Wiseman and Lord Shrewsbury. The latter wrote in defense of her in an English newspaper, *The Morning Herald,* and in the English Jesuits' magazine, *The Month.*[2]

Louise Lateau lived all of her life (1850 to 1883) in her native village, Bois d'Haine, Belgium. At sixteen she nursed cholera victims in the parish when all others, even the members of their families, deserted them in terror. More than once she carried bodies to the graveyard and

[2] It will be of interest to many to know that the late Monsignor Joseph Rainer, one-time rector of St. Francis Seminary at St. Francis, Wis., was acquainted with Maria von Moerl, of whom he was a townsman. Another who knew this stigmatist was Father Adalbert Inama, O. Praem., pioneer missionary in Sauk and Dane Counties, Wisconsin.

buried them. At eighteen Louise became an ecstatic and stigmatist, but continued to help support her poor family by sewing. An ecclesiastical board of inquiry and many physicians saw her in her agonizing Friday ecstasies of the Sacred Passion and established the fact that for twelve years her only nourishment was weekly Holy Communion and three or four glasses of water each week. She never slept during this time, but spent the nights in prayer and contemplation while kneeling at the foot of her bed.

In 1929 Baron Brion de Chapois brought to Konnersreuth a cherished piece of linen stained with blood from the stigmata of the sufferer of Bois d'Haine. When this was placed on Therese Neumann's hand during a pause in an ecstasy of our Lord's Passion, Resl began to tremble. The trembling became a violent shaking, the moans mounted almost to a scream. These were the signs by which the stigmatist of Konnersreuth testified to the genuineness of such relics. Father Naber, writes Von Lama, said that Therese Neumann had declared genuine the blood which stained the linen and all the occurrences at Bois d'Haine in connection with Louise Lateau's stigmatization.

Having in common the marks of one or more of the wounds which Christ bore on His sacred body, stigmatists differ in the number of stigmata and in other aspects of their extraordinary state. Some have been known to suffer the pain of wounds without having visible marks of them. This was true of Sister Maria Fidelis Weiss, in whom the stigmata were traceable only by the pain they caused when touched.

In some instances, the marks of the wounds disappeared, for a time or permanently, at the request of the stigma-

tized person, who wished out of humility to escape the
attention which visible stigmata almost invariably involve.
This was true of two stigmatized St. Catherines, of Siena
and de Ricci, and a number of other bearers of the
wounds. Some stigmatists bore marks of the five wounds,
but no others. Some had only the stigmata of the crown
of thorns. Indeed, Therese Neumann would seem to bear
the marks of more wounds than any other stigmatist of
whom we know. As we have seen, in addition to the stigmata most often bestowed, those of the hands, feet, and
side, she bears the marks of the scourging, of the cross's
pressure, and of the thorny crown, and in addition there
is the flow of blood from her eyes.

The stigmata of St. Francis have been described as "of
a character never seen subsequently: in the wounds of
feet and hands were excrescences of flesh representing
nails, those on one side having round black heads, those
on the other having rather long points which bent back
and grasped the skin."[3] As we know, the hand stigmata of
the Konnersreuth sufferer appeared at first on the upper
surfaces, then gradually deepened until the hands had
been pierced through to the palms.

Bearing in mind the description of the seraphic
Assisian's hand wounds, let us consider the further development which these wounds underwent in the hands
of Resl. Dr. Louis of Versailles tells us that when he
took hold of the left hand, which had been cleaned and
seemed to him to be marked exactly the same as the right
one, he examined the stigma carefully at close range. He
found in the center of the back of the hand a sort of

[3] *The Catholic Encyclopedia*, Vol. XIV, p. 295.

crust that was, however, like no ordinary scar or scab. It did not have the dull, grayish appearance of the dried scab or scar of a wound. It was reddish-brown in color with a shining appearance like that of old wax. The whole formed a regularly rounded, domelike object from the edges to the center. He noticed impressions as of a modeler's knife or of the hammer of a smith on malleable iron. All in all, the perfectly formed crusts appeared like artificially made foreign bodies placed upon the skin. But there was something which forbade any suspicion of fraud, and that was the aspect of the skin about the stigmata. Between the crusts and the normal skin, along the delicate edges, there was a transitional zone, formed by a white scarlike edging, plainly lighter in color than the bordering skin, approximately one millimeter wide and delicately wrinkled.

In the ball of the hand Dr. Louis found traces of blood which had escaped because any but the most gentle cleansing causes intense pain to this sensitive part. The wound in the palm seemed to have a crust of the same substance as that on the back of the hand, divided sharply from the edges, somewhat roughly round in thickness, longer than wide and slightly pointed. It is about one and one-half centimeters long, lies at an angle, the pointed end directed up and outwards, the other, blunter end in the middle of the hand. The scarlike border is less apparent and narrower than on the back of the hand. And then this French physician declares that these stigmata have doubtlessly the form of a *hand-wrought iron nail* that penetrates the hand from the back into the palm, where the point is bent over by hammer blows.

A priest-author who saw Therese's hand wounds in 1930 wrote that there seemed to be in this instance a gradual formation of positive stigmata out of negative ones, as in the case of St. Francis of Assisi, who bore not only the marks of the Saviour's wounds but also a representation of the nails.[4] Parallels — of which we have never seen even the slightest hint — would be the formation of a lance tip at the stigmatist's side wound, of thorns around the head, or of whip lashes where the marks of scourging appear.

Resl of Konnersreuth has a special devotion to the traditionally first stigmatist, and there is a deep, appealing kinship of the spirit between these two wound bearers. Like St. Francis, Therese has an abounding affection for birds, animals, flowers. Like him, she has an artless soul, a childlike character. And now her hands, like his, bear inexplicably produced replicas of the nails which once pierced the hands of the divine Redeemer. Soldiers formed an escort of honor for the stigmatized Poverello on his last journey back to Assisi. In our days, soldiers have visited Konnersreuth, and paid homage to the stigmatized peasant woman of Konnersreuth. But in the thirteenth century comparatively few, even in Umbria, saw what God had wrought on the body of Francis. Now, though Konnersreuth is a small, out-of-the-way village, thousands upon thousands have made pilgrimages to her home and have seen the marks of the wounds in Therese Neumann's hands.

In A.D. 1224 it is not probable that many doubted or

[4] Fahsel, Helmut, *Konnersreuth: Tatsachen und Gedanken* (Berlin: Thomas Verlag, 1932), p. 35.

had to be told why God had put "the signet of Christ" on the body of St. Francis. Today, however, an incredulous "Why?" is inevitably on the lips and in the minds of a very large number. The first prayer of the Mass on September 17, set aside by the Church to commemorate the stigmatization of St. Francis, begins as follows: "O Lord Jesus Christ, who, when the world grew cold, didst renew the sacred marks of Thy passion in the flesh of the most blessed Francis, to inflame our hearts with the fire of Thy love. . . ."

As to the stigmatization of Therese Neumann, a broad stream of eloquent explanation has flowed from the pens of men who went to Konnersreuth with humble hearts, unbiased minds; or, having come doubting and prejudiced, had their eyes opened and their minds and hearts set free. Herr von Lama says that the world which had been warmed by the ardor of Francis became lukewarm again and cold in its faith in the Crucified and in His work, the Church. Heresies led many into apostasy, then to denial of Christ as the Son of God, and finally their descendants sank into a new paganism, "so that it was as though the Saviour had never come." Therefore God, in His own way and using human beings as His instruments, drew the attention of men back to Himself again and again. In His mercy he renewed the fire of His love in the flesh of favored men and women, bestowed upon them the marks of His sacred wounds, in order to inflame the hearts of so many who do not care to know anything about Him.

The stigmata are bestowed not only, nor even primarily, to reward seraphic souls for their burning love of God.

They are bestowed for the sake of others, of as many as may be reached by their message. Archbishop Teodorowicz of Lemberg sees certain connections between the events at Konnersreuth and humanity in these days. Universal hate dominates instead of love. Men are experiencing the shattering of all hope, of civilization, and live in constant fear. "The cross of Christ has been rejected and the emptiness that arose in the hearts of men is filled only with doubts. Mankind is beginning to doubt itself. It is longing secretly for the cross that it has rejected." In a day when humanity is bereft of all nobler sentiments, "a human body appears covered with wounds, bathed in blood, but in a magnificent spiritual state." In a day when Bolshevism, contemner of all spiritual values, has made materialism its one tenet of belief, its one idol, God sends this phenomenon as a warning call. "The dam of time is broken, and the bloody passion of Christ flows in powerful streams into the present. The passion of Christ is once more accomplished in the consciousness of the stigmatized, even as in the long ago. It makes its appearance, withdrawn from time in everlasting value and everlasting life. This suffering goes on, not as something past, but present."[5]

Many others voice the same conviction, saying that at Konnersreuth this has come to pass: All have been brought face to face, in a soul-stirring manner, with the fact that Christ the Son of God exists; with the fact that He, *propter nos homines et propter nostram salutem* (for us men and for our salvation), suffered and was crucified

---

[5] Teodorowicz, Josef, *Mystical Phenomena in the Life of Therese Neumann,* trans. by Rudolph Kraus (St. Louis: B. Herder, 1940), p. 508.

and died. And as believing Catholics they deem it an exceedingly great grace to have been permitted to see the fact of the Redemption, which took place in the gray antiquity of two thousand years ago, renewed as a personal experience.

CHAPTER 5

The Twenty Years' Fast

NEXT to her stigmata, the total abstinence of Therese Neumann from food and drink attracted the greatest interest of her soldier visitors, as it had of all earlier visitors. It has been the subject of controversy since it began, and it continues to baffle men of medicine, physiologists, psychologists, all who insist upon none but a materialistic explanation.

The term *total abstinence* is often used to mean abstinence from intoxicants, without reference to other liquids or solid food of any kind and in any quantity. To fast means to deprive one's self of food to a greater or lesser degree. Therese's total abstinence means that she takes neither liquid nor solid food in even the smallest quantity.

In earlier days, many of the faithful practiced what was called the Black Fast during Lent. Only one meal a day was eaten, and that meal contained no flesh meat, fish, eggs, or butter. The dry bread and water diet is one of the most severe mortifications that penitents can impose upon themselves or that can be meted out to prisoners. But during her fast since 1927 Resl has not eaten even one meal a day. She has not eaten even one small piece of bread once a day, once a week, once a month, or once a year. She has not drunk even a teaspoonful of water, coffee, tea, wine, milk, or medicine once a day, once a week, once a month, or once a year. In September, 1947, it was twenty years since any natural nourishment of any kind passed Resl's lips, and for years before 1927 she had eaten very little food and taken almost nothing to drink.

After a prolonged alimentary disturbance in 1923, when she was unable to retain solid food, Therese's nourishment consisted solely of flour pap and tea. At Christmas time of that year she was unable, for twelve days, to swallow so much as a drop of water. Dr. Seidl of Waldsassen declared that the swallowing muscles were paralyzed. Since that time, now nearly 24 years, the stigmatist has taken no solid food; and since the fourth week of September, 1927, not the slightest amount of liquid nourishment. Up to that time, she took only a small amount of water so that she could swallow a tiny particle of the Sacred Host in Holy Communion.

Therese Neumann is by no means the first in the Church's history to abstain completely from food and drink far longer than it is possible according to nature to be without nourishment and escape death. A few men who make exhibitions of themselves manage at times to go foodless, or almost so, for sixty days, which seems to be the utmost limit. Fakirs, who fall into a deathlike sleep, can fast for longer periods, but this often ends in death if the fakir is not awakened in time. Hunger strikers undergo an excruciating ordeal and, if they persist, die.

Exceptions are stigmatists and such chosen souls as Saint Nicholas von der Flüe, called Bruder Klaus, who lived for twenty years without eating food. His home was in Unterwalden, Switzerland, and he was canonized on May 15, 1947. And not only do these exceptional men and women live without eating or drinking, but they are also in good health, physically and mentally fresh and vigorous, not the miserable, half-dead beings such as the exhibitionists, fakirs, hunger strikers, victims of starvation — all who voluntarily or perforce go foodless for what is, in comparison, a short time indeed.

Among her predecessors as stigmatists, as listed by Dr. Imbert-Gourbeyre, none is known to have abstained from all food and drink longer than Resl of Konnersreuth. Among the abstainers have been St. Lidwina of Schiedam, Blessed Angela of Foligno, St. Catherine of Siena, Blessed Elizabeth de Rent, Dominica Lazarri, and Louise Lateau.

In a book dated 1874, we are told that when Louise Lateau became stigmatized it became impossible for her to eat or drink anything on the Fridays of her ecstasies. On other days she was able to take a small amount of nourishment, but with some difficulty, and gradually all desire for food vanished. On March 30, 1871, the vigil of the Feast of Our Lady's Seven Dolors, Louise was able for the last time to take natural nourishment without suffering from the attempt. To please her troubled mother and in obedience to the command of her pastor, she tried to eat and subjected herself to this ordeal for some months. Finally it was admitted, reluctantly, that she needed no natural food, that all efforts to eat or drink caused her to suffer, and that her complete abstinence did not detract in the least from her health and cheerfulness.[1]

---

[1] August Rohling, *Louise Lateau, die Stigmatisierte von Bois d'Haine* (Paderborn: Ferdinand Shoennigh, 1874), pp. 67, 68.

Happily, no such ordeal was forced upon Therese Neumann. Of course, when they discovered that she ate less than the most rigorous Lenten rules, or the discipline of the severest religious order might prescribe, it caused worry and wonderment to her family, particularly her mother; and amazed all who became aware of the fact.

The wonderment increased when she took no food or drink whatsoever. This led to a request by the Bishop of Regensburg that Therese submit herself to a period of medical observation. The request was for a fifteen-day observation, for specialists in these matters considered such a period sufficient. They asserted that hunger might possibly be borne longer than that, but a complete fast of two weeks without taking any liquid nourishment was not possible. Resl's father agreed to comply with the episcopal request, and so from July 14 to 28 inclusive, in the year 1927, Therese was under the observation of four Mollersdorfer Sisters, members of a nursing order, who came to her home. They were placed under oath by the Regensburg ordinariate before and after the observation. All were well qualified for the task, and carried out with the most scrupulous care the directions of Dr. Seidl, the medical supervisor.

The directions were very strict and carefully calculated to meet every possible contingency. Therese was not to be left alone for a single moment, day or night, whether at home, in church, or out of doors. For this reason, even her customary confession was foregone. The Sisters were to bathe Therese, but with a damp cloth instead of a sponge. The water for mouth washes was to be measured and remeasured before and after its use. The water given to Resl so she could swallow the Host was to be measured by the Sisters before it was given to her. Periodic weighing of the body, taking of the pulse and temperature were prescribed. Blood smears were to be made during the Friday ecstasies and compared with a blood smear from the ear lobe taken on another day, after which the hemoglobin content was to be determined. According to the *Münchner medizinische Wochenschrift* supplement, No. 46, 1927, the directions went so far as to demand that "All excretions — urine, vomit, and stools — must be gathered, measured, and weighed, and immediately sent to the physician for analysis."

Professor Ewald of Erlangen, an opponent of any supernatural explanation of this phenomenon, admitted in a brochure on Konnersreuth that the keenest and most relentless attention was given to the matter of food throughout the period of observation. Despite the constant alertness, it could never be ascertained that Therese Neumann took nourishment or attempted to take it. The professor claimed that the stigmatist ought to have lost weight heavily, but such was not the case. She did lose considerably (3 to 8 pounds in a few days is no slight loss) following the days of ecstasy, but regained this in the course of the same brief period. Without taking food or drink she gained 5 to 6 pounds, so that at the conclusion of the observation her weight was the same as before.

Dr. Ewald draws attention to the fact that about 400 grams of water are taken from the body daily through exhalations. In 200 days (at the time, approximately the length of Therese's abstention) the amount would be 80 liters (or 80 kilograms). It is to be especially noted

that to meet the demands of exhalation is a purely physical process and almost totally independent of the constitution of the individual. To the loss in this manner must
be added that which accompanies the bleeding, perspira-
tion, etc. "Therese ought long since to have been dried
up like a mummy. But she is fresh-looking and lively, has
saliva, and moist mucous membrane. One may indulge
in the most fantastic imaginings, a prolongation of
metabolism as in hibernation, or fakirism — though Therese does not hibernate, but moves, speaks, reads, writes
letters, goes about — this poundwise increase in weight
simply cannot be explained; for nothing can come from
nothing."[2]

Dr. Seidl, who had been Resl Neumann's attending
physician since at least 1918, testified under oath in a
Munich court case on April 15, 1929, that there could be
no question of Therese having taken any nourishment
during the period of observation. He mentioned the fact
that, attached as she was to birds and fishes, she was not
allowed even to empty the aquarium. He maintained
flatly that the abstention of all nourishment by Therese
Neumann was a fact, which he had not the least reason to
doubt. He added that since September, 1926, the stigmatist
took no nourishment at all, not even a bit of water, as
she had at the time of the fifteen days' observation.

On January 24, 1930, again under oath in court, Dr.
Seidl stated that he was convinced of Therese's total abstinence, saying he believed in it because of the trustworthiness of the mystic and her parents, which is a guarantee.

[2] Lama, von, *Further Chronicles of Therese Neumann*, (Milwaukee:
Bruce Publishing Co., 1932), pp. 120–122.

The Waldsassen physician said also that the abstinence cannot be explained naturally.

Another upholder of the genuineness of Resl's complete fast is Dr. Fritz Gerlich, the author of an exceptionally detailed and scrupulously objective account of the Konnersreuth phenomena. He quotes Dr. Ewald as saying that "throughout the observation period there was the greatest and most intense attention," and that the instructions regarding bathing, mouth water, etc., were strictly observed. "Despite the strictest watchfulness, it could not once be observed that Therese Neumann, who was not alone for one second, took any food or tried in any way to take anything. The bed of the one observed was not only examined with the utmost carefulness at the beginning of the observation, but it was made each day not by a relative but by the Sisters. Neither the physician — Dr. Seidl — nor the Sisters were of the opinion that any mistake in observation could be admitted in regard to the taking of nourishment."[3]

The second volume of Dr. Gerlich's work is devoted entirely to an examination of Therese Neumann's trustworthiness, *die Glaubwürdigkeit der Therese Neumann.* Therein he declares that the observation period was not enough for him. He was constantly on the alert during his sojourns in Konnersreuth, a total of several months, seeking at least some indication which might lead him to discover some deception, conscious or unconscious, on the part of the stigmatist. "The daily contact gave me many an opportunity for wholly unobserved insights. Despite this I

---

[3] Gerlich, Fritz, *Therese Neumann von Konnersreuth* (Munich: Verlag Joseph Küsel und Friedrich Pustet, 1929), Vol. I, p. 132.

did not succeed in finding the slightest evidence that could give me cause to doubt Therese Neumann's assertions regarding her abstinence from nourishment. I am authorized to make the same declaration for Father Naber and Professor Wutz. Naturally, this declaration expresses only the conviction to which we have come. One may accept it or not."[4]

After the observation period some experts, still insistent upon finding a natural explanation, complained that the fifteen days' time was not long enough. But the "sincere scientific circles" consulted by the Bishop of Regensburg had assured him that no one could live two weeks without eating or drinking. Dr. Höhn, writing in a magazine published by Dr. Gerlich, says that "Since Dr. Deutsch demands a period of four weeks for a new observation of the stigmatized, another word would be in order here about the length of the fifteen-day observation by the Sisters. After consulting experts, the Ordinary of Regensburg agreed to this. Celebrated physicians with a philosophy of life entirely different from his examined the records made by the Sisters very critically; and they came to a conclusion completely different from that of Deutsch. The Sisters' daily record, according to Ewald, was kept conscientiously, exactly, without prejudice, and with sound judgment."[5]

Some physicians made the objection that hunger experts could easily subsist without food for fifteen days. Granting this, and even that some of them might manage to live thus for sixty days, the fact still remains that "it is

4 Gerlich, *op. cit.*, Vol. II, p. 382. Dr. Franz Wutz of Eichstätt, a specialist in Oriental languages.
5 *Der Gerade Weg*, Dec., 1932.

not possible for a person to be without liquid for fifteen days." Every known hunger expert has drunk water during his fast. Before the exhibition, it is agreed what drink it shall be, and some of the experts have a preference for mineral water. "We see, therefore, that the limitation of the observation by the Sisters was made with the knowledge of the known fact that the foodless body finding itself in a state of hunger will resist with absolute intolerance the shutting off of a supply of water."[6] But Therese Neumann's foodless body was not in a state of hunger, had no need or desire to resist with absolute intolerance — or ever so mildly — the absence of any liquid food.

While the controversy waged, the official organ of the Regensburg Diocese published a statement on October 4, 1927. The kernel of this official episcopal declaration was as follows: "During the fifteen-day, day-and-night uninterrupted observation not the least taking of nourishment occurred. Nor was Therese Neumann abed at all times, but was usually up. Completely puzzling was the fact that, despite the absolute fasting, twice after not inconsiderable losses of weight there followed approximately the same gains in weight. An observation in a clinic could not have had a more successful result."[7]

Of course, the naturalistic opponents were not satisfied with this declaration. There arose a clamor for another examination, in what those who demanded it were pleased to call a "neutral clinic." One at least asked that the observation be made far removed from the stigmatist's

[6] Teodorowicz, Josef, *Mystical Phenomena in the Life of Theresa Neumann*, trans. by Rudolph Kraus, p. 339.
[7] Witt, Leopold, *Konnersreuth im Lichte der Religion und Wissenschaft*, Vol. I, pp. 314, 315.

present surroundings and from her home. There was a stubborn refusal to accept the plain conclusions of the fifteen-day observation, and an implication that a different result might issue from a longer observation in an "atmosphere" other than that of Therese's home, by other than Sisters, under the direction of another than Dr. Seidl, a Catholic man of medicine who refused to deny the possibility of a supernatural explanation.

Yielding to the insistent demand, the Ordinary of Regensburg declared a willingness to take cognizance of the request. However, Resl's father stoutly refused to grant his permission. He was motivated by love of his afflicted daughter, by a justified suspicion as to what might be her treatment in a so-called neutral clinic, and perhaps he had heard what had been done to Louise Lateau. And Therese Neumann, though she had reached her majority, held herself in conscience bound to obey her father.

On September 30, 1927, the anniversary of her death, St. Thérèse of Lisieux appeared to Therese Neumann, for the first time in the garb of a Carmelite nun, and told the stigmatist that she would henceforth be in no need of earthly food.

CHAPTER 6: Food Indeed

THE secret of Therese Neumann's abundant life despite her complete abstinence from all earthly food is revealed in her statement that she is sustained by a heavenly food, the Body of her Eucharistic Lord.

On Palm Sunday evening, 1930, the third year of absolute fast, Father Härtl asked Resl if she was hungry. "You know very well that I do not eat," she answered. The curate of the village church then asked, "Do you wish to be greater than the Saviour? He ate when He was on earth." Therese smiled and said: "The Saviour can do all things. Or do you not think He is all-powerful?" Turning to the other priest present, Father Helmut Fahsel of Berlin, she declared with great earnestness: "The Saviour sustains me. He said, 'My body is food indeed,' so why shouldn't it be actually true for once, if He wills it?"

Resl, like other mystics before her, is sustained in life by the supernatural, the heavenly nourishment of Holy Communion. This is true of quite a number of stigmatists, among the more recent ones St. Gemma Galgani, who died in 1903. It is said that she lived solely by Holy

Communion, but tried to prevent this fact from becoming known, being always careful to give the impression that she took ordinary food.

The Holy Eucharist being Therese's only sustenance, and her whole spiritual life being an ardent love of the crucified Christ whom she always calls the dear Saviour (*der liebe Heiland*), it is not at all astonishing that she yearns to go to Communion, that her reception of the Blessed Sacrament has a refreshing, revivifying effect upon her whole being, and that when the space between Communions is prolonged there should be a marked change in her demeanor. Her customary Franciscan joyousness gives way to a sense of depression, so deep and mysterious is the union of Christ's suffering and the Holy Eucharist as represented in the lives of stigmatists.

Archbishop Teodorowicz says that "They receive as a mark of honor the wounds of Christ on their bodies; but no less wonderfully are their souls enriched in a particular manner, so that they possess an exalted desire for the Holy Eucharist in an extraordinary way, beyond all natural explanation. Even as their wounds are the witnesses of Christ's suffering, so is this extraordinary Eucharistic sense a confirmation of the presence of the Eucharistic Saviour on the altars of their souls."[1] Therese has this perception regarding the Most Blessed Sacrament to such a degree that she can distinguish between consecrated and unconsecrated hosts, and can perceive unerringly whether or not the Sacred Species are reserved in any church she passes.

[1] Teodorowicz, Josef, *Mystical Phenomena in the Life of Theresa Neumann*, trans. by Rudolph Kraus, p. 308.

Görres tells us that Juliana, a Cistercian nun, often noticed from afar how the Sacrament of the Altar was removed from the Church of St. Martin at the close of divine services and that this caused her to be sad. Cassetus, a Carmelite monk, was once put to the test. The Sacrament was removed from the usual place on the high altar, but the sanctuary lamp was left burning there. Cassetus did not genuflect before this altar, declaring that our Lord was not present there but in another place where no light burned. Though not a stigmatist, St. Francis Borgia had this faculty. When he entered a church he was drawn to the place where the Holy Eucharist was enshrined, even when there was no external sign of Its presence. Juliana Metles of Norfolk is said to have distinguished one consecrated host from among thousands of unconsecrated ones exactly like it.[2]

Father Härtl was present again in Resl's room after the Midnight Mass on Christmas of 1930. "She felt . . . in a manner that cannot be explained naturally, the nearness of the Eucharist before It was brought to her. . . . While lying in bed, she described exactly how the pastor (Father Naber) was taking the Blessed Sacrament from the tabernacle to bring her Communion. She described vividly his coming to her home. The road was icy and she saw how carefully he walked and made a little detour." Father Naber tells how, because he stopped en route to visit a parishioner who was sick, he was delayed in arriving at Resl's home. She knew of this delay and suffered because of it. When the pastor finally reached her room, she said

2 Görres, *Christliche Mystik* (Regensburg: Manz, 4 vols., 1836–1842), Vol. II, p. 120.

in her childlike manner to her Eucharistic Lord, "Oh, Saviour, you treated me unkindly today!"

When Therese travels to places where there are both Catholic and Protestant churches, she can perceive at once in which ones the Real Presence abides. Once, passing through a strange town, she stopped suddenly and cried out, "The dear Saviour is here!" *(der liebe Heiland ist hier!)* The building before which she stopped was not a church, but upon inquiry it was found to be a house chapel in which the Blessed Sacrament was reserved. She perceives the presence of the Sacred Species in those who have received Holy Communion a short time before, and recognizes priests though they come in the attire of laymen, because their consecrated hands have held the host which is her only sustenance. She is keenly conscious also of the continuing Eucharistic presence within herself. The usual duration of this awareness of the Divine Presence is about twenty-four hours. On Holy Thursday and Good Friday it lasts forty-eight hours. Mystical suffering, however, sometimes shortens the time by two hours.

In one instance it was possible to confirm the presence, entirely intact at 7 o'clock in the evening, of the small particle of the Host which Resl had received in the morning. Another phenomenon connected with this phase of the stigmatist's life is that as soon as the Sacred Species have dissolved within her, she feels an interior physical pain and her body begins to grow weaker. Her yearning for Holy Communion grows more intense, and she even breaks into loud complaints, saying: "Oh, Saviour, why have You forsaken me? Come, Saviour, come!" St. Teresa of Ávila declared that an ardent longing for Holy Communion was a special sign of the mystical life. Therese Neumann expresses this longing often during her ecstasies, and the pain she suffers when the Presence ceases shows its intensity. Sometimes, in the ecstatic state, she can scarcely contain herself when the moment of Communion nears and will in her eagerness stretch out her arms and even tug at the stole or surplice of the priest who is about to place the host on her tongue.

Intimately connected with Resl's abstinence from all natural nourishment and her intense desire to be united with her Eucharistic Redeemer is one of the most extraordinary phenomenon of the Konnersreuth case. This is the ecstatic Communion, minutely described in the lives of earlier mystics, among them St. Catherine of Siena. Its peculiarity is that the host, placed upon the tongue of the ecstatic, disappears immediately.

Dr. Gerlich describes an ecstatic Holy Communion of Therese as follows: "When the priest came around the corner of the altar with the ciborium, Therese, upon looking at the host, fell into ecstasy and showed the utmost desire to go forward to meet the Saviour, from which she was prevented by the arms of her prie-dieu which were locked on both sides. Her spirit glows, her eyes lighten. Her hands are somewhat outstretched, and her feet are in motion. Her whole body is somewhat raised, as if she would stand up. The pastor advised me to kneel directly in front of her so that I could look directly into her mouth. This is what happened. As the host came nearer to her, she opened her mouth wide and put her tongue out somewhat. She held her hands folded on her breast. The priest laid an entire host on the tip of her tongue and stepped back immediately. She drew her tongue back a little, upon which the host was lying, but only so far that the tip still touched her lower lip and covered the teeth of the lower jaw. Thus I could see the back part of her tongue and her gums. Suddenly the host disappeared. Therese then stuck her tongue out quite far for some time. Her mouth was wide open. She had not closed it since first opening it. From the first moment that she opened her mouth she did not make any motion of swallowing. The host could not be seen in the hollow of her mouth nor on her gums, both of which were plainly visible to me. After some time spent in the most intense concentration, she began to speak ecstatically and did so for a long while."[3]

Another eyewitness, Father Hermann Joseph of the Friars Minor Capuchin, writes: "I was in Konnersreuth on May 24, the Friday before Pentecost. No Passion ecstasy took place that day, but instead I had the good fortune of witnessing an ecstatic Communion, something which few are privileged to see. It will hardly be possible for me to clothe in words what I saw. It was too beautiful. During the parish Mass I was helping out in the confessional until the Mass was about to end. Then I went into the sacristy and was standing at the vestment case about to vest for the next Mass. Suddenly the door was opened very forcibly from the outside. Involuntarily I turned my head. I beheld a countenance so full of pain and interior sorrow, such as I had never seen before, not even in the dying. The eyes reminded me of a person parched with thirst using up his last bit of energy to reach the fountain of

[3] Gerlich, Fritz, *Therese Neumann von Konnersreuth*, Vol. I, p. 167.

water, before he sinks down exhausted. It was Therese Neumann coming to receive Holy Communion. She probably was in an ecstasy, because she saw neither me nor anyone else. It was an ecstasy of the nameless yearning and interior abandonment by God with which she is always overcome when the species of her former Communion disappear. When she passed through the sacristy I watched her every movement most closely. I do not think that I was ever so critical in my attitude as I was during the two days I was in Konnersreuth. Respectfully, she genuflected behind the altar.

"The sacristy is in a wing that was built behind the altar, so that when the door is open the rear of the altar can be seen. She sat down in the armchair that was placed there for her because of her weakness. There is an indescribable tenseness in her, it shows in every action, but there is nothing ungraceful or hurried. Now she is more herself and her face bears the usual expression. She motions to the altar boys to close the door behind her so she cannot be seen by others while she is receiving Holy Communion. Silently they obey. I opened the door ever so quietly and sat sidewise where I could see everything, unobserved by her. I wanted to see her in an ecstatic reception of Holy Communion.

" 'I do not know,' the pastor had said. 'whether she will see the Saviour today.' This occurs only when she has passed the night in expiatory suffering. Then she can receive an entire host, although ordinarily she swallows a small part with difficulty. The parish Mass was over now and the pastor took his time, even though his little lamb was almost passing away with longing for the sacred food.

I almost felt like begging him in sympathy to hurry. First the children were dismissed in order, and I do not know what else was done in the church. Only then did he put on a surplice and stole and finally appear at the corner of the altar, holding the white host above the ciborium. Although she was tiredly leaning over the kneeling-bench before, now she sat upright with her hands respectfully folded, waiting in adoration.

"He nodded to me to come close to Therese's chair for the most sacred moment. This I could easily do without being noticed by her. I knelt alongside her, about a step from her, so that I could see and observe everything. The priest came a step nearer. Therese in a rapture opened both arms wide and stretched them toward the Sacred Host. Her eyes were not directed to the host but to a Figure which I could not see. She can see the Saviour Himself, the Risen One, whom I see only under the veil of bread. Fully a minute, if not longer, the priest stood still and I used the time to calmly and carefully see and observe all as well as to impress it on my mind.

"Even today the picture is clear in my memory. It is a picture so beautiful that no master could reproduce it. Every line of it is of supreme nobility. On looking at that countenance, I was forced to think of the place in Holy Writ where it says of St. Stephen, his face was 'as if it had been the face of an angel' (Act 6:15). It was no longer the face of Therese Neumann. It was an entirely different one, showing the veneration of a creature for the greatness and majesty of its Creator. The expression was one of helplessness and resignation. And yet, what royal dignity!

It is like the reflection of what she sees. Truly, this countenance shines! But no, I am convinced that it is only the indescribable beauty of the expression on this face that makes it appear so to me. Again the words of Holy Scripture come to mind: '*Quia fecit mihi magna, qui potens est, et sanctum nomen ejus!*' A living Magnificat. That sums it up.

"Now the priest raises the sacred host to make the Sign of the Cross. Therese folds her hands and opens her mouth. Not yet, she must wait again. She waits submissively, but her intense desire is touching. And now, '*Corpus Domini nostri Jesu Christi.*' She bows her head in adoration while the priest makes the Sign of the Cross over her, and again she opens her mouth. I watch closely to see if I can note the disappearance of the host, of which so much has been written. But I see nothing. She closes her mouth too quickly. However, there is not the least indication of swallowing to be noted."[4]

Father Fahsel describes Therese's ecstatic Communion succinctly: "Her arms are raised and she gazes in the direction in which the Sacred Host is being held in the hands of the priest. While he says the remaining prayers she looks up with a blessed smile as if transfigured, and then down. I asked her afterwards why she did this and she answered: 'I see the Saviour as a radiant figure. Then the radiance becomes a flame which comes upon me and enters my mouth. I know nothing more, am wholly absorbed in the Saviour.' It is striking that she looks down with particular attention. She explains that she sees

4 Teodorowicz, *op. cit.*, pp. 315, 316, 317.

the wound marks of the Redeemer's feet in a special effulgence."[5]

Still another wonder-awakening phenomenon is Therese Neumann's reception of the Holy Eucharist without the ministration of a priest. Görres tells us of a Communion of this kind by St. Catherine of Siena. Angels brought Communion to the Jesuit boy-saint, Stanislaus Kostka, and nearer our time is the case of Blessed Imelda. This little girl yearned to receive her Eucharistic Lord and when this desire was denied because of her tender age, heaven itself intervened.

A Communion of Resl's without the service of a priest is described by an eyewitness. The stigmatist was undergoing vicarious suffering for a dying woman. Suddenly ecstatic, she opened her mouth and folded her hands on her breast, as is customary with her after receiving the Sacrament of the Altar. It was found that the consecrated host intended for her was missing from the chapel in the house in which she was then staying. At another time, when Father Naber brought her the Holy Eucharist, Therese told him that she had already gone to Communion. A priest, in a place several hours' distant by rail from Konnersreuth, noticed that one of three consecrated hosts had disappeared from where they were reserved in his private chapel. He made this astonishing and disquieting discovery on the day and at the hour in which Therese had told her pastor that she had already communicated. Two of the hosts had been given to communicants, the third had remained because the one for whom it was intended had been unable to receive that morning.

[5] Fahsel, Helmut, *Konnersreuth: Tatsachen und Gedanken*, p. 137.

Archbishop Teodorowicz says that Therese's attitude toward these extraordinary phenomena is completely calm and objective, almost as if such supernatural happenings were natural occurrences. She is convinced that her ecstatic Communions come from no merits she may have but are given to her out of the superabundance of God's goodness, and says so emphatically. But the effect of her miraculous Holy Communions is plain to all who have been privileged to be present. The first thing noticed is the physical strengthening which follows these receptions of the Bread of Heaven, the Food of the Strong. Often she is in a most pitiable condition immediately before the reception, particularly if she is suffering expiatory pain. Her face looks small, her cheeks are sunken, and there are dark shadows under her eyes. She scarcely manages to seat herself in the armchair behind the altar. But how all changes after she receives Holy Communion! One must agree then with Father Naber when he said on such an occasion: "I don't know, but Resl seems to be getting younger!"

Father Fahsel, who tells us this, also holds to the opinion that the abiding Real Presence in Therese throughout the day after her Communions gives a special power to her gift of discerning objects and spirits. Her whole demeanor, too, seems in harmony with this extraordinary phenomenon. Despite her genuine, deep humility she shows a certain self-esteem and a need for the strictest cleanliness. "For the Saviour's sake one must clothe one's self properly and act properly." This priest believes, too, that the bodily weakness which comes upon Resl when the Sacred Species are dissolved within her is so intense that, apart from the yearning which leads to the spiritual suffering of the Dark Night of the Soul, one would at

length be morally bound to give her Holy Communion
as Viaticum. He is convinced that if this were not done,
Christ Himself would come to her in sacramental form
without a priest.

Father Fahsel reports that once, when he was about
to give Communion to Therese, he saw that the host was
already on her tongue. She explained the matter to him,
to save him from anxiety. She was very weak and yearned
intensely for the Saviour. Her desire was further increased
because she was aware that two scoffers who ridiculed the
Blessed Sacrament intended to forcibly enter the sacristy.
Her longing reached such a high degree of intensity
that Jesus came to her before the priest could administer
Communion. Father Fahsel adds that then he recalled
how, shortly before he went to the altar, someone tried
roughly to open the sacristy door.

The mystic of Konnersreuth lives healthily without
taking any earthly food, and also with scarcely any sleep.
As her physical health is not impaired by her complete
fast, so it is maintained in a splendid condition without
sleep which all others need so much. Resl's nearest relatives and her spiritual director report that her sleep has
diminished to no more than two or three hours each week.
A strengthening repose comes to her in the state of prepossession during the ecstasies, but this lasts at the most
only twenty minutes, and throughout this time her soul
is intensely active in mystical union with God.

An exception is the sleep following upon Therese's
Good Friday visions of Christ's suffering. Then, during
Holy Saturday and the night before Easter Sunday, she
is granted repose, but throughout this mysterious sleep she

is united with the Saviour in an exceptional manner, while her body shares the rest of His body in the grave. After this sleep, the agony of the stigmatist's bleeding or of her vicarious suffering vanishes completely and her body becomes fresh and well again. During the Friday Passion ecstasies Therese invariably loses several pounds in weight. After the repose in the state of prepossession she recovers this lost weight, regaining all of it by the following Saturday evening or Sunday.

It has been observed, too, that Therese falls into a sort of half slumber after her visions which lasts only three or four minutes each time. Then she opens her eyes and is more alert and lively than ever before. The tiredness after the visions is caused, no doubt, by the spiritual and intellectual strain of these experiences, during which she follows intently and shares in all she sees.

Even unbelievers and pronounced skeptics who have seen Therese Neumann's vigorous activity when she is in her normal state are heard to say that if her absolute fast is a fact, then she is a continuous miracle. But to form a correct judgment it is necessary to consider all of the phenomena: stigmatization, abstinence from food, sleeplessness, ecstatic Communion, and the ecstasies themselves — those awe-inspiring, soul-gripping spectacles which have made Konnersreuth a place of unforgettable experiences.

Therese Neumann be-
came an ecstatic when she received the first of her stigmata
in 1926. Not all ecstatics have had the marks of the
wounds, but all true stigmatists have been granted ecstasies
and received their stigmata while enraptured. This has
been the rule to such an extent that any stigmatization
lacking the marvelous complement of ecstasies would be
suspect, not the kind proposed to us for veneration.

When a chosen soul is granted a supernatural ecstasy
it becomes rapt in contemplation of divine things, is
caught up into a most intimate union with God. The
mind is completely absorbed in this contemplation, and
during the time of ecstasy the bodily senses are in abey-
ance, but the soul remains fully awake. The spirit dominates the flesh absolutely.

Christian ecstasies are spontaneous, whereas the pagans
tried to bring them about by physical and psychological
means. The ecstasies of Christian mystics have as their
goal the possession of God through the spirit and not
through the senses. They are received humbly as gifts of
grace. Such truly supernatural raptures increase the sanctity of those to whom they are granted, are always in-

spiring and elevating, bestow new light and strength, and are never debasing or scandalous like the induced trances of pagan mystics.

In addition to her usual, normal state, three other states of consciousness are clearly discernible in connection with Therese Neumann's ecstasies. Her normal state "corresponds completely with the usual state of a normal person and shows nothing extraordinary. Therese shows herself to be a bright, lively, and friendly person of ripened spirituality." It has been noticed, however, that Resl's normal state underwent a gradual change, or a development "which extends beyond the usual concept," and the opinion has been expressed that this is due to the sacramental presence within her of the Saviour after she has received Him in Holy Communion.

The first state other than the usual, normal one, is that of exalted rest, an ecstatic sleep or coma during which the divine Redeemer uses the sensory organs of the stigmatist to manifest Himself to men. Father Naber has written: "Despite her many sufferings, Therese is remarkably fresh and lively. When things get desperate, when it seems she cannot possibly carry on, the Saviour makes Himself felt and she enters into an 'exalted' state of rest (as she called it recently), from which she awakens newly strengthened. In this condition the curtains of the past and of the future and of great distances seem to be lifted for her. The Saviour permits her to see hidden things."

Dr. Gerlich, in his careful, detailed analysis of this ecstatic state, describes the condition as follows: "It brings Therese Neumann the feeling of being united with Christ and of sharing in His blessed happiness and omniscience, in so far as He permits this. And meanwhile Therese's body rests and gathers new strength. . . . She lies, generally, on the pillows, her hands crossed over her breast. However, I have also seen her raised up and gesticulating. Her eyes are as a rule closed. Her body serves as a means of expression. She speaks with the utmost animation while in this condition of exalted rest. The transition to the normal state is accompanied by the outward signs of awakening, generally with loud yawning, stretching of the limbs, and so forth, as people usually awaken from sleep.

"When Therese returns to normal she remembers nothing of what she speaks in this state. On the contrary, she takes it for granted that she has been sleeping and is astonished when one tells her the contents of her speech. Occasionally the third party, the one who hears her conversation while in the state of exalted rest, is distinctly commanded not to tell her, when she returns to the normal state, what she said, as she need know nothing about it."

It has been noticed that Resl seldom speaks High German while in the state of exalted rest, preferring to use the Upper Palatinate dialect of her native section, which is somewhat difficult for many to understand. While in this condition she also addresses all persons, regardless of rank or station in life, with *"du,"* the German familiar form of *you,* whereas ordinarily she is careful to use the polite form *"Sie."*

While in this ecstatic sleep Therese is able to look into the souls of men, to know their pasts and to some extent their futures, and has a knowledge of people who are not present. She is careful, however, to say: "Remember, it is not I. The Saviour lets me know this." And no matter what is asked, no matter who asks it, her answer in this state is always given with astonishing quickness and certainty, as could be expected only from one who has a complete insight into all the circumstances. No diplomat could be more careful.

When her counsel is asked in an important matter, she begs our Lord for a suffering before making a reply, as if she wishes to merit the heaven-granted ability to convey an answer that is correct and helpful. Her conversation concerns spiritual matters almost exclusively. She explains with theological exactness such matters as the relations of faith and science; tells an inordinately proud scholar to consider the dying words of Socrates: "I know that I know nothing"; declares that magnetism, crystal globes, and clairvoyance are of themselves natural things, but that the devil is prone to use them; says that the lost grave of a medieval abbess will be found, but not that of a saint.

In closing his report on this condition of the ecstatic, Gerlich says that the more comprehensive his study became, the more his experience and observation compelled him to admit that for him at any rate "the explanations thus far offered do not suffice. Nor is it this alone that makes such a strong impression on me. The deepest impression has been the result of Therese's absolute conformity to the Christian religion. Never before have I seen such a perfect fulfillment of the demands of Christianity."[1]

A German priest-author defines two kinds of "rest" in

[1] Gerlich, Fritz, *Therese Neumann von Konnersreuth*, Vol. I, p. 172.

Resl's state of exalted repose. One is the rest of sleep
which refreshes the ecstatic in a most extraordinary way
after her physical suffering has become unbearable as a
result of the Friday ordeal of the Passion, or when she
has undergone expiatory suffering for others. The other
is a sleep during which the soul of the mystic is united
with God in the height of contemplation and ecstasy, rests
in Him, as it were. This "rest" occurs almost invariably
after she has received Holy Communion.

As to the adjective "exalted," this is explained by telling
what happened when, on one occasion, Father Naber
received no answer from Therese while she was in this
state. When he repeated his words, she opened her mouth
and he heard the words: "You cannot speak with Resl
now, she is sleeping." Then to his amazement words
continued to come from her mouth, certain brief directions regarding designated visitors. He marveled because
he was suddenly addressed as "*du*," and because the words
came with such certainty as indicated unqualified authority. It developed that words of guidance were given to the
parish priest while his spiritual child was in this state.
For example, he was told: "Tomorrow one will come
(and he was described in some detail) who must be allowed
to see *me*." Or, "At 8 o'clock this evening *I* will have a
vision." Again, "At 4 o'clock this afternoon *I* will begin
to suffer." Therese never knew, afterward, what had been
said in this way, but what was said always happened.

The second state is that of prepossession, which occurs
mostly during the pauses of Therese's ecstasies, and which
follows the last ecstasy of the Sacred Passion on Fridays.
In the beginning, this state was not sufficiently distin-

guished from that of exalted rest. It is marked by the absence in Resl of any *scientia acquisita* (anything learned or acquired through experience), although her personal consciousness remains. As far as her natural knowledge is concerned, she is like a child, and her mode of expression reflects a childish age. But only the manner of expression, only the *form* and not the *content* of what she says, is that of a child. Perhaps the purpose of this is to eliminate all that might disturb or change the objectivity of what the ecstatic sees, what is said to her, and what she repeats. As in the state of exalted rest Therese remembers nothing of what she says while in this state.

When the state of prepossession begins, Therese is no longer the enraptured seeress of the completely ecstatic state, but she describes minutely what has been impressed upon her, and answers questions, though she is still absorbed in what she sees, and participates in it actively. It is a more than natural state, in the opinion of Von Lama, who saw how the stigmatist had the power of hierognosis; that is, of discerning true from false relics. The mental concepts of the ecstatic are those of a child, her manner of expression conforms to such concepts, says this writer.

"My presence during these conversations of a soul of childlike piety with its God is among the most touching and beautiful experiences I have had. . . . The ecstatic is unable to comprehend such simple concepts as brother, sister, parents, numbers. In describing the discovery of the true cross, she declared that the cross of Jesus consisted of four parts, after the longer section had been cut into two. She said, 'one and one and one and one.' 'That is four?' asked Father Naber. 'Four? I do not know. There

was one and one and one and one.' The cross of the penitent thief had three parts. 'Three? I do not know. One
and one and one.'

"All who have listened as I have for hours to conversations such as these will agree that Therese's childlike
condition is not self-induced or feigned. It seems to be a
charismatic gift accompanying the ecstasy and perhaps it is
based on the fact that, by emptying the memory of all
else, it prevents anything learned at school or later from
being added to the vision content. Therese is probably
intended to be a connecting link between the actualities,
sensibly seen by her, and us; between the actualities of
nearly two thousand years ago and us, who live in the
twentieth century after Christ's birth. Again we are reminded of Our Lord's expression of thanks to His heavenly Father for having revealed to the children and to the
simple what He hides from the wise ones of the world."

When Resl begins to speak in this semiecstatic state
after the Friday ecstasies, she tells her compassion for the
Saviour, "and her speech changes into a long and moving
prayer, a peasant's presentation of all sorts of petitions
for relatives and friends. For herself she makes no request,
save only that she be permitted to die. And all she says
has this childlike refrain: 'But You are smarter than I
am and You will know how to arrange everything for the
best.' "

Finally, there is the third exceptional state, that of
complete ecstasy, which begins with the condition familiar
to mysticism, the *raptus,* an instantaneous surrender of
the whole being to a supernatural compulsion. This comes
upon Therese Neumann with startling abruptness, as

once when she was in the midst of describing her gold-
finch. "Often in the middle of a word," says an observer,
"in the midst of activities which carry Therese's thoughts
far from spiritual things, the ecstasies break upon her like
the storm of a primeval world. They tear her from the
pillows into postures which are often, physically speaking,
violations of the law of gravitation, and draw her arms
forward and upward. Only the play of the features, now
animated and readable beyond all precedent, shows what
she is undergoing."[2]

Sometimes Father Naber would try to divert the attention of Resl on Thursday evenings, to prevent even the
shadow of possibility that suggestion might play any part
in producing the ecstasy, but he never succeeded. The
rapture came upon the stigmatist with complete sudden-
ness, no matter what she might be doing or saying at the
moment. During one of the pauses, which interrupt the
ecstasies of the Passion and usually last from ten to fifteen
minutes, Therese receives Holy Communion.

On one occasion, the acolyte who carried the priest's
surplice and lantern back to the church had scarcely gone
when the stigmatist was hurled from her pillow. Half
lying, half sitting at an acute angle, in a position that
would normally be extremely tiring and almost impossible, she stretched out her arms. They were steady, as
though supported in mid-air. Her fingers, especially her
thumbs, were turned slightly inward, and the marks of
the wounds glowed with ruby freshness. Her arms moved
back and forth occasionally, almost imperceptibly. Her

[2] Aretin, Erwein Freiherr von, in *Einkehr*, supplement to *Münchener
Neueste Nachrichten*, Aug. 3, 1927.

face, framed in the white headcloth which was now streaked with blood from her eyes, was raised. Her posture was like that of a blind man who listens intently, who has no earthly orientation, and who lives and sees only in his soul.

Therese is wholly indifferent to and beyond the reach of any exterior influence during the several separate visions in her ecstasies. She answers no questions and responds to no touch of the hand. A fly which alighted on her closed eye was allowed to remain, and she gave no sign of being aware of it or annoyed by it. In the village square below her room the funeral procession of an old soldier passed with a blare of martial music. The windows rattled, but Resl neither moved nor gave a sign of having heard it. When she awakens, she falls back on the pillow and answers questions. Her consciousness, however, is limited to what she has just seen in the vision, and she is totally ignorant of what is yet to come.

Therese Neumann's appearance while in ecstasy is like a celestial reflection of the stupendous interior drama or heavenly joy in which she participates. "External ecstasy in its beauty and emotion is the window through which by means of corporeal actions the internal hidden flame of love can be observed," says the Archbishop of Lemberg. Especially during Resl's visions of the Passion can the witness plainly see how the flame of love burns with pitying love for the Man of Sorrows, and how she actively shares in the suffering of Christ crucified. But the mystic reflects otherworldly happiness when the ecstatic vision is a joyous one. The memories of such inexpressible visions may well be the cause of the Franciscan joyousness of her whom Father Schenk, the Jesuit chaplain, has called "a person who is truly happy, possibly the happiest person in the whole world."

HOW truly Therese Neumann participates in the suffering of her divine Redeemer when she follows Him from Gethsemani to Golgotha in her ecstatic visions, is told by a large number of those who have seen how the Sacred Passion is then mirrored in her face, in her gestures and words, and in her whole being caught up in a rapture of love and pity.

An American bishop relates how he and a priest of his diocese, having been ushered into the small upstairs room of the Neumann home, "found little Theresa sitting in bed in an upright posture with her hands extended, her eyes two pools of blood. From them there issued two streams as wide as my two fingers, pouring down over the cheeks and onto her white dress. The headcloth was completely saturated with blood, and you could see the certain strong points where the blood seemed to issue, indicating the place of the thorns entering into the head of our Lord. As she sat back with that terrible pain, her whole face writhed in such tremendous agony as I have never seen in all my life, her hands extended, the wound marks glowing a bright inflamed red, it appeared she was trying to help our Lord as she saw Him pass through the various scenes of His Passion.

"At the moment we entered she was seeing Our Lord meeting with His blessed Mother on the way of the cross. Oh, how she held out those hands of hers to Christ and to His blessed Mother! You could read in her face the Passion, the scenes that her soul was witnessing. As far as she herself was concerned, she was absolutely dead to the world. There was neither sight nor feeling nor sense in her body at the time. . . .

"And then suddenly she started back and the visions came to her again. She raised her hands aloft. Her lips became gray and parched. Her tongue came out seemingly parched, as she cried out, 'I thirst!' Her eyes rolled in agony as she went through the scenes of that ordeal of the crucifixion, and at last, when the final words were spoken, she crumpled back on her bed, the picture of tortured death, if ever there was one. Oh, what a sight! Never, never have I witnessed anything like it. It will be printed on my memory to the longest day I live. I saw the Passion of Our Lord as I have never dreamed of it, as I have never meditated on it in all my life before."[1]

A non-Catholic gives his impression: "As I recall her on the next morning, she is a picture which no one who has ever seen will ever forget. The form of the girl rises out of the pillows, the upper part of her body in an oblique position, her arms outstretched pleadingly. The wounds of her hands burn. Her face is racked with ceaseless pain. She wrings her little white hands as if her heart

[1] Schrembs, Joseph, *Amazing Teresa Neumann* (Cleveland: Catholic Universe–Bulletin, 1928), pp. 12, 13.

were breaking. It actually does break. Long since, her heart's blood has saturated all bandages. This girl weeps blood. Blood streams over the distorted face out of painfully closed eyes, at first only a few light drops appear, but finally from both eyes two wide streams flow over the entire extent of her cheeks. A thousand impressions pass over her distorted face, terrible events carve themselves in this fearful, tense, attentive countenance. Her body jerks. She experiences the scourging of the Lord. And suddenly, as the enemies of Christ place the crown of thorns on His head, wounds appear on her head and dye the headcloth red. Tortured, she reaches for her head, as if to try to draw out the thorns — and this again and again."[2]

Dr. Von Weisel, who is not a Christian, testifies: "I gaze and gaze. Before me, upright in the bed, is a picture of woe. An aged face stares enraptured into vacancy, paying no attention to us standing about. The mouth is half opened, the hands are stretched out helplessly as though seeking something. They clutch at the vacant air, and are withdrawn with a gesture of despair, to be crossed over the breast. And the eyes — never before had I seen such eyes! No hysteric, no insane person has such eyes: agonized, horrified, her swollen, blood-encrusted lids are turned to her visions, which only these closed eyes behold. These eyes see more than our open eyes. And red, red drops of tears are on her cheeks. About ten o'clock [a.m.] there were six or seven long stripes of blood on the left cheek; on the other cheek the number was much less. But in the afternoon both eyes are equally submerged in

2 Reismann, Dr., *Der Tag*, Sept. 6, 1927.

blood; blood streams are coagulated on the cheeks and chin and jaw, down to the neck. Bloody tears color even the chemise. The ecstatic weeps blood. And on her outstretched hands, which are colorless as faded wax, gleam two red marks in high relief: the nail wounds of the Saviour!"[3]

A later testimony is that of an American woman after her pilgrimage to Konnersreuth in 1934: "Theresa was not in the room where she had received us the previous year, but in a smaller one adjoining. She was half sitting, half lying in a narrow white bed, close to the wall which had a high railing attached to the outer side to prevent her from falling out during her paroxysms. Pillows of snowy whiteness were piled high behind her, and she was covered by the usual thick white-down quilt (almost like a small feather mattress) that is used in those European countries. On the wall by the bed hung a crucifix, surrounded by several reliquaries containing, no doubt, relics of her favorite saints. There was also the framed photograph and blessing of the Holy Father. Against the wall opposite the door, and near the bed, was an altar large enough for the Holy Sacrifice. A cage of birds was hanging in the corner farthest from Theresa's bed. It was partially covered to keep the little songsters quiet and only an occasional twitter was heard. Except for this there was deathly stillness in the room.

"Laymen were on their knees; the priests stood at the foot of the bed. It was twelve o'clock and Theresa was in the beginning of the agony on the cross! Her hands were extended, the stigmata plainly visible — her dear face had

---

[3] Weisel, W. von, *Vossische Zeitung*, Aug. 16, 1927.

lost all semblance of beauty and was drawn and agonized. The white cloth covering her head was beginning to be saturated with blood. The six stains were becoming a deeper red as the minutes passed. Her eyes were pools of blood and black streams clotted her cheeks and throat down to the neck of her white gown. Her face was ashen and the lips drawn over the teeth, while her head turned from side to side in intensity of pain. Her hands twitched and quivered, moans came, and sighs of anguish. One could imagine, as the hours went by, how the snowy whiteness of her garments and her bed of suffering would be dyed with the crimson tide, flowing in emulation of the Blood of the Blessed Savior on Calvary. My first thought as I dropped upon my knees in the presence of such suffering was, almighty God alone has the power to perform such a miracle."[4]

One who knew Resl and Father Naber intimately declares that when he saw the stigmatist in one of her Passion ecstasies he knew it was Therese Neumann, but not because anyone would see in this almost ghostly being the young woman who had chatted so blithely with him and others the day before.

The picture which Therese presented was, for him at least, not overwhelming though it was immeasurably impressive. What was overwhelming was her participation, for it was concentrated beyond her upon the object of her vision. He allowed the spectacle to work its way with him, and it led him to the place where Therese was then dwelling and to see what she was seeing, the Way of the

[4] Brennan, Elizabeth Marable, *Visits to Konnersreuth* (New York: Paulist Press, 1936), pp. 27–29.

Cross in Jerusalem. He experienced what Therese experienced. In that moment the Saviour was all. The surroundings, even the people, including Resl, were unimportant accompaniments, trivial matters, as Therese herself said when questioned during pauses in the ecstasy.

Time disappeared for this spectator. All was in the present tense and the day of Calvary was the apex of all ages. The ecstasy, he saw, was a complete one, a wholly, exclusively supernatural vision. Therese was withdrawn from the entire created universe, and the entrance of several pilgrims did not disturb her in the least. The stigmatist struggled for breath and moaned faintly, but when she was asked if the pain was intense, her answer always had reference to the suffering Redeemer. For Him were her touching, childlike whispers of compassion, never for herself.

An insight into the unsparing realism of Therese Neumann's ecstatic visions of the Passion, and her sharing in it, is given by this chronicler when he tells us that toward eleven o'clock in the forenoon on this Friday, Therese began to complain that it was unendurably hot, for at that time the procession of the cross-bearing Saviour, as she followed Him, had passed from the shade of the houses in Jerusalem! At a quarter to twelve there was the cry, "The crucifixion begins!" And the crucifixion of Christ did in truth begin in the mirror of Therese's enraptured vision. Under the agony of the nailing her hands twitched continuously and her thin fingers contracted. Her tongue sought in vain for moisture on her lips; her head fell forward and her mouth licked the sponge raised to it, but turned aside with a gesture of bitterness. Then Resl's head was raised, in an attitude of listening, to the left; that is, to the right side of the Saviour and to the thief crucified there. Her pain faded for a moment, for she heard with visible joy the words of the penitent Dismas: "Lord, remember me when Thou shalt come into Thy kingdom!" Then she hearkened toward the crucified Redeemer, to catch His reply, but turned suddenly with an angry look away from the curses of the impenitent thief, the "bad man" as she calls him when asked about this character in the sacred drama.

At twelve-thirty o'clock a change came over Therese's face. Only pain had been mirrored there, but now the countenance turned ashen gray, almost gray blue, the cheeks became cavernous, the face was drawn lengthwise making the mouth smaller. Involuntarily the man's lips formed the words, "My Lord and my God, up there on the cross, forgive me, too, for Thou didst die for me and my sins!" That, he says, was truly an act of perfect contrition and that alone would have been ample recompense for all the inconveniences of his journey to Konnersreuth. He concludes his report by telling how a last terrible spasm passed over Therese's body, from her feet upwards. There was a final summoning of the last remnants of strength — and in the same instant, so quickly that he could not catch the details, Resl fell back upon her bed, as heavily as a stone, and her hands dropped to the coverlet, for it was consummated.

To answer the question, "Does Therese Neumann suffer actual physical pain in her Friday ecstasies?" it is enough to see her as these witnesses saw her, when she beholds her dear Saviour scourged, crowned with thorns, crushed to earth under the weight of the cross, crucified. "She is no despairing, helpless witness of the terrible tragedy on Calvary, like the Mother of God, the holy women, or even the timid, fearful Apostles. She is personally active, a Joan of Arc in the presence of her Saviour. She does not fear the enemies of Christ, who are rejoicing over Him. She does not despair for a moment as to the success of her attempt to rescue Him. That she has formed a plan to save her Master through flight, that she has also brought in assistants for the accomplishment of her plan of saving Him, is attested by her words, 'I know a shorter way.' She points out the road with her fingers in the air, with all of its turns and deviations. . . . Her decided tones reveal that she wants to enter into the minutest detail of carrying out her plan of safety for Christ."[5] This is true because of the peculiar character of the ecstatic visions, in which Therese does not know what is going to happen, clings to the hope that *the Dear Lord* will not actually die. And the climax of her sorrow comes when she is forced at last to admit that all her hopes were in vain, all her brave plans fruitless. What Therese of Konnersreuth feels in that moment is summed up in her pitiful, agonized words, "Oh, I cannot help the Saviour!" "Oh, Saviour, what have they done to You!" And her physical suffering, excruciating as it is, is merely a shadow of the torment in her soul. "Therese coendures the suffering of Jesus. She is present as an eyewitness. Because of her tender love for the Redeemer she shares everything with Him, she feels the mistreatment and the pain, experiences them to

[5] Teodorowicz, Josef, *Mystical Phenomena in the Life of Theresa Neumann*, trans. by Rudolph Kraus, p. 193.

the utmost possible degree in soul no less than in body."[6]

According to the stigmatist, the designation of the semi-ecstatic states, those of exalted rest and prepossession, come from the Saviour. They are provided for her by His merciful consideration, as periods of relief after the tension of the ecstatic suffering, lest otherwise the heart be burdened beyond its strength.

It ought to be borne in mind that all the suffering of Resl in union with her suffering Redeemer is voluntary. She has accepted this as her life's vocation, to share the agonies of the Passion out of love for Christ and in expiation for the sins of men. She is no longer in the elementary classes but in the graduate school of the cross. As far back as November, 1925, after one of the astonishing cures of her earlier years, she was told by St. Thérèse of Lisieux: "You shall still suffer very much, but you must not be afraid, not even when the interior suffering comes. It is the only way that you can co-operate in the saving of souls. But you must die more and more to self." And on another occasion: "Only through suffering can you perfect your character and realize your vocation of sacrifice, and thereby assist the priest. More souls are saved through suffering than through the most brilliant sermons."

It is interesting too, and worthy of note, that Therese's ecstatic visions are orientated according to the Church's liturgy. Almost all the contents of the visions conform to the liturgical season in which they take place. Her visions of the Passion do not take place on Fridays on which the Church does not especially commemorate the suffering

[6] Franzmathes, Dr., *Der Segen von Konnersreuth* (Kirnach-Villingen: Schulbrüder Verlag, 1929), p. 36.

of the Redeemer, such as the Fridays between Christmas and Ash Wednesday, those between Easter and the Feast of the Sacred Heart, and those which fall within the octave of a major feast. Singularly, on the Fridays of the pre-Lenten season she sees the Passion only to the taking captive of Jesus after the Agony in the Garden.

The bleeding of Therese's stigmata conforms to the liturgy, too. Only on Good Friday do they all bleed. Those of the head, hands, feet, heart, and shoulder bleed on the Fridays of Lent, when the bleeding of the eyes takes place too. On ordinary Fridays the bleeding is confined to the eyes, heart, and head.

In the spring of 1947, Therese suffered from both asthma and a rheumatic condition in her right shoulder. "This appears to be the reason why she was relieved of the pain she underwent in previous years on that part of her body, the one where our Lord suffered the heaviest burden in carrying the cross to Golgotha. It has happened frequently that Theresa was relieved of a corresponding mystical suffering whenever she went through some physical disability."[7]

Finally, the pain caused by the stigmata is measured somewhat by the liturgical period. Thus, during Lent the stigmata of the feet cause her more pain than at any other time, so much pain that she cannot leave her home.

So intimate is the mystic's connection with the liturgy and so complete her response to its spirit that when the Church rejoices, she experiences an exceptional feeling of physical well-being, and is in a joyous mood. She shows

[7] Jordan, Dr. Max, in National Catholic Welfare News Service report. Konnersreuth, Apr. 21, 1947.

this especially on the three great feasts: Christmas, Easter, and Pentecost. She cannot hide her happiness then and has been described as like a child excited over Christmas gifts or some other simple joy. On Saturdays she often looks younger and healthier than usual, in anticipation of Sunday's spiritual happiness.

VISITORS to Therese Neumann's home before the war saw the large number of letters she received daily from many parts of the world. It was impossible for her to read them all, or to answer those she did read. Often she asked one of her brothers or sisters to help open the letters, and she read as many as she could at night while the others slept. But because all of the letters are not read and answered does not mean that the petitions in them are ignored by the stigmatist. She answers as many appeals as she can, for helping others even at the cost of intense suffering is a part of her heaven-sent vocation, as announced to her by the Little Flower, St. Thérèse of Lisieux.

When asked how she managed to help all who appeal to her by letter and how she selected from the vast number those which were to be heeded, Therese answered that she commended all of them without exception to the all-merciful heart of the Saviour. "We ought to pray for everybody, and especially for those who ask for our help or tell us their troubles," says the mystic of Konnersreuth. "I am not forced to suffer. If I wished, I could say 'I will not suffer,' and it is surely true that nobody likes to undergo pain. But when I know that it pleases the Saviour, then I am ready. Then I say 'Saviour, let the pain come.' And He lets me know for whom I suffer and how it ends."

Therese's expiatory suffering for others is purely physical when she offers to undergo the pain of sickness that another may be cured. It is both physical and spiritual when the one for whom she suffers is afflicted in soul as well as in body. It is purely spiritual when the one for whom she suffers is the victim of spiritual but not physical sickness. It lasts from a few hours in some instances to three or four days in others, and has even lasted for years; in one instance for more than eight years.

A strange aspect of the stigmatist's voluntary, pity-prompted ordeals for her fellow men is that she is afflicted with the others' physical ailment; and in the case of spiritual disorders she shows the effects of human sin and weakness. One afternoon her father called Father Naber because something out of the ordinary was happening. Resl lay on the sofa and acted in a way completely foreign to her character. She and the whole room reeked with the odor of alcohol. It was found that at the time someone in another town was suddenly freed from his addiction to alcoholic drink.

A letter to Father Naber from this man related how he was about to commit suicide when he saw the form of Therese Neumann before him. The apparition lasted a half minute. He was deeply stirred, gave up the idea of killing himself, and found that he could master the craving for alcohol. Resl endured exceptionally severe spiritual suffering at the time this man at some distance from Konnersreuth was close to death at his own hands.

The mystical ordeal called the Dark Night of the Soul overwhelmed her and in the midst of alcoholic odors, symbols of the man's besetting sin, she felt a complete disgust with life, such as one feels who is about to "end it all."

One of the earlier instances of vicarious suffering on Therese's part dates back to the Christmas of 1922. She heard that a young man's dream of becoming a priest was threatened by a throat disease. Thereupon she spoke to our Lord: "Dear Saviour, I lie here and can do nothing, so it doesn't matter, I will take this suffering upon me too." The touching quality of the words is heightened when heard in Resl's dialect: *"Heiland, i lieg do un' kann nix tun, da macht's nix aus, i nahm dös Leid noch auf mi."* The seminarian was cured at once and in his stead Therese became ill with the throat trouble. From that moment she was unable to take solid nourishment. "Here we see how certain phenomena of mysticism are interrelated. For the discontinuance of solid food probably served the purpose, as we may surmise, of preparing the body of Therese for stigmatization and for the stigmatic's mystical relationship to the Sacrament of the Altar."[1]

As a result of the throat trouble she was unable to swallow an entire host, when in the normal state. While she was in the state of exalted rest she was told that she would continue to suffer until the seminarian was ordained and had offered up his first Mass.

The young man for whom Therese suffered in this instance was ordained to the holy priesthood on June 30, 1931, and offered the Holy Sacrifice of the Mass for the

[1] Fahsel, Helmut, *Konnersreuth: Tatsachen und Gedanken,* pp. 94, 95.

first time in Regensburg soon thereafter. On the morning of his first Mass Therese suffered so much that she could scarcely speak. The Mass was to begin at 6:30 o'clock in the morning, and it was hoped that the suffering would stop soon afterward. However, it did not cease until 9:30 o'clock, and later it was discovered that the young priest had not begun his first Mass until 9 o'clock. The suffering stopped at the moment the neo-presbyter pronounced the words of consecration. After that, the stigmatist was able to receive a whole host at Communion.

Therese's father also benefited by the vicarious suffering of his daughter's part. In 1923 he was the victim of severe attacks of rheumatism, which was a serious matter for him in his work as a tailor. Resl asked to be allowed to suffer in his stead, and he was cured instantly. Her left arm thereupon became stiff and the constant pressure of the left hand against the breast caused a sore, the scar of which remains. Resl also suffered for her youngest brother, John, then a student at the gymnasium in Eichstätt. He ceased to be troubled with head grippe which interfered with his studies, but she suffered from head grippe until long afterward. She is always ready to undergo pain for her loved ones. One must not conclude, however, that because of this her relatives are spared all sickness. On the contrary, there has almost always been some illness among them.

Therese sometimes suffers during one of her Passion ecstasies for one who has sinned grievously, or for an unbeliever, as soon as that person enters the room. And those concerned feel instantly that something is happening in their souls. One incident of this kind has to do with a man who was a visitor in the village. After a Friday ecstasy Resl asked her father to summon the man whose name and address she gave him. The man was amazed when he was called by name and told that Therese Neumann wished to see him. He was a so-called free-thinker, who had come to Konnersreuth with the intention of staying a number of days and perhaps incidentally seeing the stigmatist. When he came to her room in response to the summons, he experienced a vehement spiritual stirring and at the same time Therese's suffering increased.

A number of times, traveling in an automobile beyond Konnersreuth, Therese pointed to buildings and said, "Sins are committed there. I wish to atone for them," and soon it was apparent that she was suffering. She stated that the sins were against the Sixth Commandment, and in some instances, at least, it was possible to establish the truth of her statement regarding the buildings.

On Saturday, July 26, 1930, the stigmatist suffered more than usual, both physically and spiritually. On this occasion she could not retain the host which she had received in Holy Communion that morning. From the handkerchief on which it had been placed and which Father Naber held in his hands, the host disappeared into her mouth, and she was instantly transported into an ecstasy. When she sank back on the pillow and the state of exalted rest ensued, it was revealed that Therese had suffered for a dying young woman. On her deathbed the young woman had confessed to sacrilegious Communions. On a number of occasions she had taken the host from her mouth, placed it on a handkerchief, showed it to others, and joined in their scoffing. The young woman had suffered from tuberculosis. Therese underwent the pain of that disease in its last stages and, in addition, endured the Dark Night of the Soul to atone for the sacrileges of the dying one.

In 1928 the stigmatist suffered for a drunkard who had poisoned himself in a fit of despair. All the symptoms of poisoning appeared on her body, the virus gathering in two boils, which were exceedingly painful. Still another example of her vicarious suffering for one close to death came in the same year, when she sacrificed herself for a woman who, converted from a loose life, had relapsed into her former mode of living. Therese knew in advance that she would have to suffer "exceptionally much," but she showed no fear as the ordeal approached.

In yet another ordeal, in 1930, Therese had a fever of 104 degrees while suffering from pneumonia. This was endured for a dying girl in the Rhineland who, betrayed at 14, had lost her faith. Therese was compelled to withstand three long hours of such temptations that had it not been for the constant spiritual support of her pastor, she could scarcely have triumphed over the fierce attacks. The girl died at 5 o'clock in the morning January 18, 1930, after having made an act of contrition. At the same moment Resl declared that a letter would come soon with good news. The letter came as she had predicted and it told how the girl had received the Last Sacraments and died a good death.

Therese suffers for groups as well as for individuals. It was observed that at carnival time in 1928 and 1930 she endured terrible hunger and unquenchable thirst in atonement for sins of drunkenness and gluttony. Vomiting

spells of the severest kind came upon her and, despite the
fact that already then she took no liquid food whatsoever,
she vomited forth a liquid that had an offensive stench
of beer, wine, and whiskey. The odor could not be ban-
ished for a number of days, even though the room was
thoroughly aired. Exasperated Herr Neumann said, on this
or another occasion, "One would think we had a tavern
here!" Resl said that if people knew how much she suffered
for them at such times, no one would ever again attend a
ball. During at least one of her vicarious ordeals at carnival time she had a vision of Christ sweating blood in
Gethsemani and beside it another of the excesses of Shrove-
tide crowds.

Besides suffering to help those stricken by disease or
in spiritual difficulties, Therese endures pain to help souls
in purgatory. Then her agony is of the soul rather than
of the body. An indescribable sadness and an intensified
yearning for the Saviour come upon her. She lies in the
bed in a state of extreme depression, her heart overflow-
ing with pity for the imprisoned soul for whom she is
suffering. One hears her moan: "Saviour, to You! Saviour,
to You!" She wrings her hands, much as she does in her
ecstatic visions of the crucifixion. Flaws in the characters
of the souls for whom she suffers are shown symbolically
by her at these times. She shows extreme concern for
earthly goods because in life the woman was greedy and
miserly, or she indulges in talk entirely foreign to her
true self because in life the object of her atoning pain was
careless of her tongue.

It has happened, too, that Therese offers up pain for
the one who inflicts it upon her. Thus, when she visited

a physician and he in his professional eagerness grasped her wounded hand roughly, she cried out, but said at once, "For him, Saviour!"

The evidences of sickness which show on or in the body of Resl when she suffers for others cannot be explained by men of medicine. It is amazing how, within a few minutes, she will show the effects of dropsy, for example, such as do not ordinarily appear until some weeks after the sickness has begun; or how she suddenly has a bloody cough, such as consumptives have in an advanced stage of the disease. Equally astonishing and inexplicable are the sudden disappearance of all evidence of illness and the complete absence of any aftereffects. She recovers in this way even when, in the course of her suffering for a dying person, she endures all the agony of a person's last hour to such a degree and so realistically that those present are almost convinced that they are actually seeing a death.

Several of the Konnersreuth conversions are attributed to Therese's vicarious suffering. She offers herself as a victim to obtain the grace of conversion for Catholics who have strayed, or to obtain the gift of faith for non-Catholics. In one instance, the pain she endured in a Friday ecstasy was applied to a Jewish merchant. This man, a former Socialist writer, was with Father Naber and Father Fahsel in Therese's room when she, in the state of prepossession after an ecstasy, pointed toward the Jew and said: "You know, there stands one who doesn't as yet belong to the Saviour, but he is a good man, he wishes to come to the Saviour and the Saviour wants him." Later, again in the state of prepossession, when this non-Christian reverently touched Resl's hand, she told him: "You seek

and seek and ponder, but you are not satisfied. You have
much but you are not contented. When you have the
Saviour you will have a great joy. Then you will have
all things."

Deeply stirred, the Jew asked, "What must I do?" Resl
answered, "You know, the Saviour will manage it all right.
I have prepared the way for you, all you need is to have
good will." The sequel is a happy one, for the Jew said to
the two priests the next day: "I do not say 'Thank you!'
but for the first time in my life I say 'Praised be Jesus
Christ!' Today I laughed again for the first time in three
months. There is a joy within me which I cannot explain.
When I went walking this afternoon it seemed to me that
Christ walked always ahead of me." Later, the stigmatist
announced that now the man believed the words of the
Saviour.

In April, 1929, while in the state of exalted rest, Therese
declared that a Protestant from Berlin would come to
Konnersreuth soon. On May 5 she stated that the Protestant would come that day and was to be brought to her.
The man had come to Konnersreuth in an agitated state,
troubled by doubts and beset by difficulties. He was present at an ecstatic Communion of the stigmatist and afterward heard these words from her mouth: "You would
please the Saviour very much if you became a Catholic."
After long pondering, during which his four children
became ill but recovered after Therese had prayed for
them, the man finally entered the Church. Therese told
him on one occasion something which she could not
possibly have learned in any natural way. After his conversion, Therese occasionally suffered for him, and each

time this happened he had had exceptional temptations
to overcome, as he himself reported.

Therese Neumann's expiatory suffering, for the living
or for souls in purgatory, is not new in mysticism, in which
it has had a prominent place, says Archbishop Teodorowicz. St. Catherine of Siena suffered for her father, and
St. Catherine de Ricci for the Medici, a powerful Floren-
tine family of the Renaissance. Other mystics who suffered
in this way included St. Margaret Mary Alacoque, Blessed
Catherine de Racconigi, and Veronica Juliani, to whom it
was said, "You are the helper of the souls in purgatory."
Imbert-Gourbeyre states that stigmatists especially undergo
expiatory suffering. When the stigmatist of Konnersreuth
has suffered atoning pain to an exceptional degree, she is
granted surcease and new strength by a vision of Christ,
followed by an ecstatic Communion; and this Communion,
"which is closely connected with expiatory suffering,
places a supernatural seal on her suffering and on the
source of it."[2]

Because it springs from her love of the Saviour and
her heroic readiness to suffer for souls whom He loves,
for whom He suffered and died, Therese Neumann's
expiatory, vicarious suffering knows no narrowing bounds.
A woman who had gone to the village school with Resl
was dangerously ill and was not expected to live. She asked
that Therese come to her. This woman had had a number
of illegitimate children by different men and her present
condition was due to an especially difficult birth. The
stigmatist, asked if she would go to a woman who had

[2] Teodorowicz, Josef, *Mystical Phenomena in the Life of Theresa Neumann*, trans. by Rudolph Kraus, pp. 380, 381.

led such a life, answered at once: "Why not? she needs intercession and help more than others do." And she went to see the woman.

Therese suffers for others with such unselfish generosity because her tender heart is glad to endure pain if, thereby, she can spare one dear to her or an unknown suppliant; and most of all, if she can help another to save his or her soul or win release from purgatory. Hers is such a love of God and love of neighbor as only valiant chosen souls achieve. Many will gladly do what they can conveniently do for others, or even at some inconvenience or cost. Not many will submit, freely, to extreme and sometimes prolonged physical and spiritual pain for others. Therese is willing and able to do this because she has through the years "died more and more to self," as admonished to do by the Little Flower, and lived more and more out of love for the dear Saviour and for all her brothers and sisters in Christ.

O F ALL the phenomena of Konnersreuth, none grips the soul of the beholder more than the ecstatic visions in which Therese Neumann sees the Passion of Christ far more vividly and completely than the most lively imagination and devout meditation could evoke from the fourteen Stations of the Cross. She mirrors what she sees so impressively that the onlooker is stirred to the depths of his being. The stigmatist is more than a spectator: she shares in the emotions of one actually present at the events from Gethsemani to Golgotha, and she partakes in the agony of the divine Victim, the replicas of whose wounds she bears on her body.

Therese's first ecstatic Passion vision took place in the Lent of 1926, when she received the first of her stigmata. The bestowal of further marks of the wounds accompanied ecstasies during which she saw successive scenes of the Passion, the trial before Pilate, the scourging at the pillar, the crowning with thorns, the carrying of the cross, and finally the crucifixion. In her village Resl's enraptured visions and the resultant pain are called *das Freitagsleiden,* the Friday suffering.

The Bishop of Koniggrätz in Czechoslovkia was one of

the many who before World War II saw Therese in the
Passion visions which begin late on Thursday night and
last until noon or into the afternoon of Friday. There may
be as many as thirty-five or forty visions, the earlier ones
brief, interspersed with periods of prepossession during
which Resl speaks and answers questions regarding what
she has just seen. At 11:30 on the Thursday night when
the Bishop of Koniggrätz was present, the stigmatist lay
quietly in her bed and was in a cheerful mood, chatting
with those about her. To judge from her appearance and
demeanor, no one would expect that acute suffering would
come upon her within ten minutes. Then suddenly, at
twenty minutes before midnight, she raised herself up,
stared forward for about three minutes, her body motionless, her arms extended. The subjects of the first, second,
third, and fourth short visions were Christ's coming to the
Garden of Olives, His prayer, and the Apostles who fell
asleep, unable to watch with Him an hour.

In the fifth vision, a smile lights up the face of Therese
because she sees an angel come to console the Saviour.
But her face quickly betrays pain when His agony causes
Him to sweat blood, and blood begins to flow from her
eyes down upon her cheeks. From time to time she
clutches at her heart, as if to lessen the pain there, and
the side wound begins to bleed too. In the sixth vision she
looks with repugnance at one who pushes himself forward
rudely, evidently the leader of the mob which takes Jesus
prisoner. After the seventh vision she speaks of the cold
and it is to be noted that later the Roman guards have
fires. As the eighth vision opens, Resl raises herself up,
stretches out her arms, smiles. She sees Judas kiss his Lord

and Master and to her this appears as a sign of friendship.
Soon her face is distorted by pain, when she realizes that
Iscariot has betrayed the Saviour. Intense agony is mirrored
in her face as she sees, in the ninth vision, how Jesus is
taken prisoner, bound, and led away. She sees the soldiers,
the servants, the healing of the ear of Malchus after im-
petuous Peter had cut it off with his sword. The hand
wounds are bleeding profusely and the bleeding of the
eyes increases as the Redeemer is led across the brook of
Cedron toward Jerusalem. She explains that "They pushed
the Saviour into the brook near the bridge. I pity Him
so much!"

Christ before Annas, the former high priest and father-
in-law of Caiphas, is the subject matter of the eleventh
vision. One of the onlookers strikes Jesus in the face. In
the state of prepossession after this vision, Resl says she
does not wish to tell what happened. She cries out, as if
in atonement for the outrage: "Saviour, we love Thee,
Thou art so good!" She insists that Father Naber make
the same declaration. The bleeding wounds cause her increasing pain. In the twelfth vision the stigmatist beholds
the hate of the witnesses against Christ in the house of
Caiphas, where Annas lives. Questioned, she describes
minutely the attire of the high priest in the thirteenth
vision, after which she exclaims: "It does not go good
with the Saviour. They give Him a fool's. . . ." (A fool's
garment?) In the fourteenth Peter denies Jesus, the rooster
crows. She describes Peter as "the one who cut off the ear."
She turns away with loathing and wrings her hands as, in
the fifteenth episode, Christ is condemned before Caiphas.
"The Saviour is tired. . . . They tortured Him so, and then

they led Him away. . . . The Saviour looked at the man
[Peter] and then he wept." In the sixteenth, Christ is in a
prison cell. "It is a dark hole. And it is cold there. He
will stay there until early in the morning." It is now almost
three o'clock Friday morning. The first nine visions filled
the first, the next six the second hour since 11:40 Thursday
night. After a two-hour ordeal the sufferer is granted a
period of exalted rest.

The seventeenth, eighteenth, and nineteenth visions
seem to concern events connected with Christ's appearance
before Pilate and Herod. In the twentieth Therese
stretches out her hands again, as if to help someone, then
wrings her hands and gazes to the left, then to the right,
full of terror. She cries out, "Saviour, gladly!" clutches at
her right shoulder and moans. She sees the scourging, the
stigmata of which appeared on Good Friday in 1929. When
the twenty-first vision begins, the mystic's white headcloth
is saturated with blood which flows from eight wounds
encircling her head. The blood streams from her eyes now
unite under her chin. The stigmata of the hands, feet,
and side bleed profusely, too. She sees Jesus start on His
way to Calvary and later describes the alleys and houses
along the route. The realism of her visions is shown also
by the fact that, when the crowning with thorns takes
place, she hears the words of derision in Aramaic, the
common language in Palestine at the time of the Passion.
She hears *"Salem, malka (je) hudaje! Salem, Mesicha!
Salem, rebhutha!* — Hail, King of the Jews! Hail, Messias!
Hail, Majesty!"

When, in the twenty-second vision, Jesus meets His
mother, Therese wrings her hands, gazes sorrowfully to

the left, cries out "Oh!" in pain. Later she says that our Lady was accompanied by John and several women. Resl managed to draw close to the Saviour and understood what He said: " *'Immi'* — My mother!" The content of the twenty-third and twenty-fourth visions seem not to have been known. But in the twenty-fourth the stigmatist sits upright, looks unwillingly to the left, her face betrays disgust, she wrings her hands in helpless agony. She sees how Simon of Cyrene is compelled to help Jesus carry the timbers of the cross. In a later description she said that Simon did not belong to the mob surrounding the Redeemer and looked different. She motioned to him to help Jesus but he did not wish to do so. Then a soldier forced him to. "He was furiously angry." The Cyrenean took hold of the beams at the bottom, so Christ still had the heavier part of the burden. Simon scolds and yells until the Saviour looks at him so woefully that the heart of the man is touched, he draws nearer and carries more of the weight, which pleases Resl very much.

The twenty-fifth vision causes Therese to clutch her right shoulder and moan. In the twenty-sixth she sees Veronica offer a sweat cloth to the Saviour, and after this ecstatic vision she explains that the "Lady" Veronica was accompanied by a young girl who carried a jar of water. Veronica owned a house and was probably rich. Jesus had cured her of an issue of blood and now, seeing Him covered with blood, she took off the shoulder cloth and held it out to Him. He pressed the cloth lightly to His face and the image became visible on it. Then Veronica returned to her home with the cloth, which was not a veil. The stigmatist added that in those days people had no pockets in their clothes but carried handkerchiefs fastened at the shoulder.

From the twenty-seventh to the thirty-fourth vision Therese sees how the Saviour falls under the crossbeams, counsels the women of Jerusalem, and reaches Calvary. In the thirty-fifth the timbers which Jesus carried to the place of execution are formed into a cross. The hill of Calvary is not high. After the thirty-sixth vision Resl says that the Saviour was filled with fear. They put Him in a sunken grave to await death. They place Him on the cross, to find out where the holes must be bored for the nails. In the thirty-seventh vision Christ is stripped of His garments and nailed to the cross. "One is stirred to the depths of his soul by the spectacle which Therese now presents. . . . Fresh, red blood gushes from all her wounds. The sight tears at one's heart. She moves her fingers as one whose hands are nailed. The whole body twitches in frightful pain. The feet twitch, as though they were being pierced by nails. Now she stretches forth her hands — toward the Saviour — and moves the fingers of the right hand. With the cry again and again of 'Oh!' she gazes in terror at what her spiritual eyes behold: the cross is raised up."

The climax nears: "Resl stares upward. The fingers twitch convulsively. The hands are folded and lifted toward the Crucified. . . . No matter how thickly the blood covers her eyes, she does not cease to look with silent agony at the Saviour. Again a convulsive twitching of the fingers and again she lifts her trembling, imploring hands upward to the cross." The Redeemer hangs on the tree of salvation between the two thieves, is mocked by the Jews, the soldiers, and one of the thieves. Therese gazes sadly upward, hears the words, "Father, forgive them, for they know not what they do." She looks with detestation to the left, where the Pharisees and doctors of the law make sport of Jesus. Then, after lying as if unconscious for a time, the stigmatist stretches her arms toward the cross again, as though she wished to cry out in her agony: "Saviour, what have they done to Thee!"

The blood flowing from her eyes has now stained the chemise. She turns to the left, as if to hear Christ say, "This day thou shalt be with Me in paradise." The thief to the right, Dismas, has repented, and this fills Resl with joy. But she points to the right, where on the left of the Saviour hangs the unrepentant thief, and folds her hands in prayer for his conversion. She puts out her arms again in a gesture of boundless sympathy. "She is like a picture of the Sorrowful Mother." Then, though it is high noon on Calvary, darkness falls. Jesus speaks: "Woman, behold thy son. Behold thy mother." John, who had been standing to the left under the cross, goes to the right to support our Lady. The cry, "My God, My God, why hast Thou forsaken Me?" is heard. Therese looks up at the cross once again, then at Mary, with intense sympathy for her, and at the Crucified with keen participation in His agony. Suddenly she extends her tongue as the Saviour cries out, "I thirst!" A soldier lifts a sponge dipped in vinegar to the Redeemer's lips. The stigmatist moves her lips, passes her tongue over them, as though she, too, would taste the vinegar. Once a happy smile plays across her haggard, bloodstained features. According to Father Naber, this was because the Saviour looked down and smiled benignly at her, whereupon she drew even nearer to the cross.

Now the climax: Resl is aware of the Redeemer's death agony. She sees how the rocks are split. Her face shows nothing but pain. The fingers quiver, the hands are quiet then for a moment, but soon move convulsively. Her uplifted face shows intense agony. But a moment later the countenance is calm, her hands quiet. She does not wring them now, but folds them in prayer. She bows to the right, hears Christ say "It is consummated!" Her head falls sideways, to the right. Death is near. The words wrung from the dying lips of Jesus are heard: "Father, into Thy hands I commend My spirit!" Therese's head sinks forward. She raises herself up momentarily, sinks back, as if dead. The mouth is half open, the lower jaw somewhat pendulous. Neither the lips nor the fingers move. Her body lies motionless as a corpse. "The one whom her soul loves is dead!" It is fifteen minutes to 1 o'clock. The ecstatic vision of the crucifixion had lasted fully three quarters of an hour.

Generally, Therese's Friday suffering ends with the vision of Christ's death. However, on Good Friday and the Feast of the Seven Dolors, three visions are added. The thirty-eighth shows the soldiers breaking the legs of the thieves, and from this sight Resl turns with shuddering; the piercing of the side of the Saviour with a lance, whereat a tremor seizes her and she sinks back upon the pillows. In the thirty-ninth, she looks piteously at the Mater Dolorosa still under the cross of her Son. She sees how the nails are withdrawn from His hands. Once the mystic said that she saw our Lady at this time sitting on a small rug and leaning on a stone. One leg was outstretched, the other bent at the knee, and in this position she received the body of Christ upon her lap. In answer to Father Naber's questioning in the state of prepossession after this vision, Therese said that those who took the Saviour down from the cross had been to see Him once at night (Joseph of Arimathea and Nicodemus); that the ladder was a pole with rungs alternately on the right and the left. In the fortieth vision, the body of Jesus is laid in the grave. Therese is aware of the pleasant odors of ointments. She gestures to show the enfolding. She told, afterward, how she saw the narrow vessel in which the ointment was brought by the "girl" (Mary Magdalen), who broke the cover so the odors could escape. The Mother of God looked indescribably lovable and sorrowful. They carried Jesus down under a hill "and I saw Him no more. . . . His head was especially bound in linen and also His hands. They had done the same to Lazarus."

After being present at Passion ecstasy visions of Therese Neumann in March, 1928, Father Mager, a Benedictine, said that the spectacle was in no way repulsive or theatrical. "I saw the Passion Play of Oberammergau. It was impressive. Hundreds wept. But it was a small thing compared with what I saw in Konnersreuth. The two cannot be placed in the same category." Another witness stated that the Passion visions were exalted, unique, and all who saw them took back home something to remember as long as they lived, be that a hundred years.

Therese Neumann told a visitor that she could not help it "that I have visions. I hold myself to be merely an instrument which God uses as He pleases according to His plans. As far as I am concerned, it would be all right if my strange wounds were to vanish today and if I had no more visions. It is all the same to me whether I have them or not. I share in the suffering of Jesus with the greatest sympathy *(Mitleid)*. The pain which I see the dear Saviour endure I feel, too. During the visions I 'see.' I am so completely alone with the dear Saviour that I could not possibly have any time to think about myself. Though I suffer at the sight of the inexpressible suffering of Jesus, I am only slightly conscious of it at the time. I experience the pain as my own and directly applied to me when the visions are interrupted and Jesus vanishes from my sight. For example, when Jesus is scourged, crowned with thorns, crucified, it is not as though I too were scourged and crowned with thorns and crucified. It is true, I suffer pain, involuntarily, and this pain resembles that of the dear Saviour. But I cannot pay any more attention to it. However, when the separate visions end and a pause comes between them, then I suffer the pain as of scourging, especially on my back. It seems to me that thorns pierce my head and I experience the pain in my hands and feet as my own. At such times I haven't headache, for example, but I feel the piercing pain of thorns pressed into my head. I grasp at the place as though I wished to pull something out; that is, the thorns."

Asked what hurts her most as she sees and shares in the Passion, Therese has said that it is her intense desire to help the Saviour and her inability to do so. This is probably expressed by her frequent stretching out of her arms in a gesture of the utmost desire. She is not aware of this while in ecstasy, knows of the stretching out only from the reports of bystanders. "During the visions I am wholly absorbed in the sight of Jesus. He alone has my interest and attention." She does not see pictures, she explains, but objects. "I see the Saviour and the others exactly and with as little effort as one sees something taking place in the street. I cannot think: I wish to see this or that especially. I do not select the objects, according to my preference, as one does in meditations. What is most remarkable impresses me most and I have no time for distracting curiosity. I do not see in the way people see what is played on a stage, nor as if that which I see was taking place far away. I see as one who is present and I do not know that I am lying in bed. If I had been present 2000 years ago I could not have seen it all more clearly nor experienced it more directly, intensely than I do now. It seems to me that what I see happens for the first time. . . . Each separate event absorbs me so completely that I cannot think there will be other events, or that I have already seen this, or that the principal parts were in my Bible history. Everything is new each time, as new as the first time." Does this explain the ecstatic's total ignorance of what is to come in her visions? Until the end she believes that the Saviour will be freed. Even on Calvary she consoles herself with saying that they merely caused Him to carry timbers up the hill, for she does not see the cross as such borne by the Saviour but as beams which are roughly put together on the Mound. "I see, hear, feel nothing whatever about me. When the visions cease, the end is just as abrupt as the beginning. Then I concern myself with recollecting

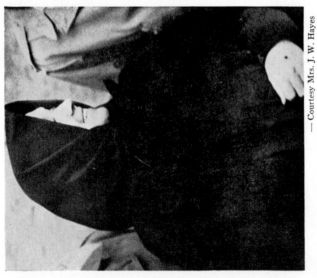

Two pictures of Therese Neumann by American soldiers.

Therese with her parents before the accident of March 10, 1918.

Bomb-riddled home of Therese Neumann.

G.I.'s viewing ruins of Father Naber's house.

Therese's brothers repairing side of her house shelled by retreating Nazis.

Refugee children cared for by Therese in Konnersreuth.

Father A. S. Carney interviewing
Therese Neumann.

Therese Neumann gathering flowers for the altar.

Therese with nephews and nieces.

Therese with Father Naber and two American guards.

what I have seen and then too my own physical suffering is felt more."[1]

A student of mysticism who has studied the Konnersreuth phenomena declares that during her visions the body of Therese Neumann is in a state of mimic ecstasy. It is in ecstasy because it no longer reacts to natural sensory stimuli, and it is mimic because it is not stiff as in the case of some other genuine visionaries, but remains mobile and carries out definite movements. The eyes follow the spectacle with lively, concentrated attention, as though unwilling to let anything escape them. Their vision is not disturbed if one passes a hand in front of them, nor even if the eyeball is touched. The head is turned as when people try to hear more distinctly what is being said. The whole course of events, all that is seen, is mirrored in the face so clearly and impressively that not even the greatest actresses could equal it. The movements of the arms, hands, and fingers indicate certain happenings with such realism that the beholders can tell at once what the stigmatist has just seen and experienced, if they are acquainted with the scenes in the Gospels.

This, says the student of mysticism, reminds him of a passage in the writings of St. Thomas Aquinas to the effect that the angels can, by moving and acting upon the human fantasy, impress upon it a picture which overflows upon the sensory organs. And because of this he is inclined to believe that the process in the visions and mimic ecstasies of Therese is as follows: A more-than-human power,

[1] Witt, Leopold, *Konnersreuth im Lichte der Religion und Wissenschaft*, Vol. I, pp. 188–191.

be it God or an angel, acts upon, stimulates an inner organ which the Scholastics call the *sensus communis* (inward central sense). The same power then carries the stimulus through the fantasy to the outward sense organs. A speaker's inner idea is transformed by his fantasy into outward sensory instruments, expression, and gesture. This is exactly opposite to the process by which a man's natural power becomes aware of outward things and then only is the idea produced through the sense organs and the fantasy.

Now, as Therese Neumann's visions are invariably accompanied by mimic ecstasy, they become an additionally persuasive sermon on faith. This is true especially of the Passion visions, for the Christian belief is rooted in acknowledgment of Christ's suffering and death, says this writer. All witnesses, believers or unbelievers, are moved mightily by this silent eloquence. And as our time has a special need of being reminded of Christ's Passion as a historical fact, one cannot but recognize the finger of God in this, especially since the case of Konnersreuth was suddenly made known to the whole world.

He points out also that the phenomena of which Therese Neumann is the center are not without precedent. He mentions only the case of Maria von Moerl in the Tyrol. Between July and September in 1833, some 40,000 persons passed through the stigmatist's room and were moved by the sight of her in mimic ecstasy combined with visions of the Passion. Many took home with them resolves and attitudes of which their pastors spoke long afterward.[2]

2 Fahsel, Helmut, *Konnersreuth: Tatsachen und Gedanken*, pp. 43, 44.

One of the interesting aspects of Therese's visions of the Passion or of other incidents in the history of the Church is the accuracy with which she sees and later describes the background, the architecture, the dress and manners of the people, and their language. As to their speech, she not only hears the vernacular of the time and place, Aramaic, but distinguishes between dialects of this tongue. One expert, who had delved into the history of the temple in Jerusalem and written a doctor's thesis on it, was amazed at the peasant Resl's wide and exact knowledge of the building.

Dr. Gerlich tells us that Therese sees buildings exactly and knows the difference between Grecian and Oriental architecture. Another writer says that drama plays a surprising part in all the details of the visions, and all these details could not possibly be known to Therese in a natural way. "When asked, she tells her story with the clarity and directness of an eyewitness. The Bavarian dialect and the primitiveness of her expression depict things and figures most naïvely. She could be really called a genius of details. She describes the form of the pots of pitch, lamps, Roman eagles, bundles of fasces — things she does not know and, because of her education, could not know. In a schematic sketch of the Last Supper in which the places taken by the Apostles are numbered, she gives immediately a graphic, pictorial description of each Apostle. I do not recount this as proof of a miracle but to show the extraordinary spiritual ability of this peasant girl (village school, ten years of heavy farm work, and eight years of protracted suffering). These things lie between farsighted vision and poetic vision of things not present but which nevertheless have the appearance of reality."[3]

Of course, it is not the incidental historical accuracy of her visions, it is solely the central core of them all, the Passion of the divine Redeemer, which compels Therese Neumann's coendurance and complete absorption. The Saviour and what He suffers are all that matters to her. That and the application of His suffering to the souls of men, whom He loved unto death, whom Resl loves because of Him, and for whose sake she surrenders herself to all the pain of her ecstasies and visions, as also to her wounds and all the circumstances of her mystical life.

[3] Natonek, Hans, *Heilige Kranke oder Schwindlerin*, pp. 41, 42.

CHAPTER 11: Visions of Joy and Glory

I
N ADDITION to the visions which correspond with the themes of the sorrowful mysteries of the rosary, Therese Neumann is granted visions which are like the joyful and glorious mysteries. These experiences of joy and glory include the triumph of the Risen Christ, His ascent into heaven, events in the lives of the Blessed Virgin Mary and other saints. They are less poignantly dramatic than the ecstatic visions of the Passion but are equally realistic and detailed. They also are reflected in the face and gestures of Therese by the mimicry which makes it easy for the bystanders to understand what she is seeing; the more so because these visions are so often in accord with a season or a feast of the Church's liturgy.

The first of these apparitions came at Christmas, 1926, about nine months after Therese's stigmatization and first ecstasies and visions of the Passion. Christmas Eve of that year was a Friday, so Resl had undergone the *Freitagsleiden* and, as midnight neared, was recovering from the exhausting strain. Only her father was with her, all other members of the family having gone to Midnight Mass. Herr Neumann sat beside his daughter's bed and read to her from Goffine's explanation of the Gospels. The church bells could be heard as they rang for the Consecration of the Mass, the father knelt in adoration, but was aroused by an exclamation from the smiling lips of his daughter. He saw how she listened as if to something as yet far away but drawing closer. Her blue eyes were large and bright with expectation, and she sat up in bed. The enraptured vision lasted a long time, even after the mother and brothers and sisters had returned from Midnight Mass. One of the brothers was sent to call Father Naber. Meanwhile Therese sank back in the pillows, as the vision ended, and was heard to say, softly, as if to herself: "Now I would be glad to die. . . . It is always beautiful there. I should like to die. It is so dull here."

After a number of attempts, Father Naber was able to establish the source of Therese's happiness by using the words, "The Christ Child has come!" At the sound of these words the stigmatist spoke, joyously: "Ah, yes, it was the Christ Child!" Then she told how she had been awakened by wondrously sweet music. The light which she had seen a number of times appeared again and a voice she had heard before and knew as that of St. Thérèse of Lisieux now spoke to her: "You are permitted not only to suffer with the dear Saviour, you shall be joyful with Him too. But remain submissive and childlike." She raised herself up and all at once there was about her another and incomparatively brighter light. "And I saw a little child above me, on a cloud as it were. Oh, it was so beautiful! I saw the child in the midst of the light. It had the most tender, rosy cheeks, not deeply red, but just a little, and the dearest of little feet. . . . The soft hair framed the smiling face in golden curls. It looked at me so mildly with its bright, deep-blue eyes. The child wore a little dress. It stretched out its arms to me and smiled at me. It was as though the child wished to come to me!"

The song Therese had heard in this vision impressed her very much, but she could not understand it. Shortly thereafter Professor Wutz of Eichstätt visited her. He spoke the words, "Glory be to God in the highest," in several languages, but each time Resl shook her head, "No, that is not it." As though doing so casually he spoke the words in Aramaic, and instantly the mystic exclaimed: "That is it! That is what the song said, but there is a little of it missing."

At the time of this vision Therese had long ceased taking any solid food. Henceforth she ceased also to take liquid food in any form.

A year later Therese Neumann had another Christmas vision. What she saw on the Feast of the Nativity and also on the three days preceding it has been minutely detailed by Fritz Gerlich, from notes by Father Naber. On December 22 she saw how Joseph, returning home from work, told Mary they must go to Bethlehem to be enrolled, in accordance with the decree of Caesar Augustus. Joseph wished to go alone, because he feared the journey would be too hard for the Blessed Virgin. She, however, insisted upon going with him in obedience to the decree, and said that God would take care of them. They prepared for the journey by packing food and other necessities on a she-ass, chosen because they needed her milk. They also took with them, packed on the ass, the cloth and poles of a tent. They left Nazareth at about

6 o'clock in the morning, Mary riding on the donkey's back and Joseph leading the animal by a leather strap. In his left hand Joseph carried a staff higher than himself. The weather was rather cold and rainy, the road rough. When night came they set up the tent near a number of trees, since there was no dwelling within reach. The ass was tied to a tree.

On December 23 Therese saw how Mary and Joseph resumed the journey at about 5:30 o'clock; how Mary walked at times, to spare the animal, and how she and Joseph became very tired, so that they prayed for help. They saw a house in the distance. The old man and old woman who lived there with their son and daughter welcomed the friendly strangers. They noticed our Lady's condition and how pale and tired she was — ordinarily she was strong and well — and gave up their meager but warm meal to the travelers. Later our Lord rewarded the hospitable old couple, for they died good deaths, heathens though they were. The boy grew up to hear John the Precursor preach and be baptized by him and then he became one of the seventy-two disciples of Christ. The girl became a Christian, too, and met death at the hands of pagans when she tried to destroy their idols.

The night between December 23 and 24 was spent by Mary and Joseph in a village inn. On December 24 they resumed the journey at 6 o'clock. The ass became tired in the afternoon, but people in a village along the route revived the animal with food without charging for it. The weather was cold and rainy. Therese saw how the holy pair reached Bethlehem about 5:45 p.m., entering by the northern gate. Bethlehem had about 1100 inhabitants at that time; the flat-roofed houses had square or round windows with grilles of wood or curtains instead of glass, and the streets were paved with large stones.

Joseph went into one of the houses, but came back quickly, somewhat downcast, and told Mary that no lodgings were to be had there. He went into another building, a long, broad one, an inn, but again he was told that there was no place for them. One of the houses was the enrollment building, but Joseph wished to postpone the enrollment until the next day, because there was such a throng waiting to be counted by the census takers. Mary persuaded him to obey the decree at once, because she knew her hour was drawing near. Once more Joseph sought shelter, but again he returned disappointed, and Mary consoled him. The last of the men to whom Joseph appealed directed him to a stable beyond the southern gate of the town and gave him permission to stay there, since he was a part owner of the building. His shepherds were among those who would later worship the divine Infant.

Mary and Joseph walked to the stable, guided by a lantern which Joseph had brought along. About 8 o'clock they reached the stable which was built on the eastern slope of a hill as an addition to a cave which formed its northern portion. The roof and walls were of wide boards, and in the wall to the right of the entrance was a small window. Joseph tied the ass to an upright beam in the farther left corner of the stable and hung his lantern from the roof. He prepared Mary's sleeping place near the right wall, spreading the tent cloth and a gray woolen cover on the ground. He made a straw pallet for himself at the left wall, using another woolen cover. The sky was beclouded.

At 11:13 p.m. on December 24, 1927, Therese was caught up in ecstasy and saw in visions the further events of the first Christmas. Her face glowed with happiness, her gestures were unusually lively, even her feet moved and her fingers sought to take hold of something. At 11:30 she sank back into the pillows and closed her eyes, to open them a minute later and begin to tell with animation all that she had seen. She was now in the state of pre-possession. "I have just been to a stable, there was a little child wrapped in coverings. I saw the little one's hands, which were very small, and its eyes, which it kept closed much of the time. The weather was cold."

Resl did not tire of voicing her delight at seeing the child, and only after considerable effort was it possible to have her continue her account. "I was in a stable of wood that leaned against a blackish-gray hill. The ground was not level and there were rocks strewn about." She stood to the left of the door, looking into the stable. An ass was tied to a beam toward the rear of the place. Asked if there was not an ox there, too, she said "No." Resl called the child in the stable *Butzerl,* a Bavarian dialect term of endearment for a baby. She said the child lay in a manger, not such a manger as is used in Konnersreuth for feeding the cattle, but one of wood resting on X-shaped legs. There were a number of other mangers. The baby lay with its head toward the rear wall. Again and again, while speaking thus in the state of prepossession, Therese asked who the *Butzerl* might be, and when she was told that the child was the Saviour, her joy grew even more intense.

Continuing her report, Therese said that the mother stood to the left of the Child and stroked His hands. Joseph was to the right, standing with folded hands, and he said something which Therese did not understand. Now Mary had her arms crossed over her breast. The Child had dark-blue eyes and curly fair hair. The straw on which He lay was very dark and stronger than theirs. (Later, in the state of exalted rest, Therese explained that in the manger there was straw only at the bottom, over which rushes were spread). Rushes were evidently the dark straw she mentioned. The lantern Joseph had hung from the roof was burning in this later vision. All through her recital her chief concern was not for the externals, the "properties," so to speak, but for the personages, most of all, of course, for the Christ Child, to whom her words always reverted.

According to the notes of Father Naber, and reported by Gerlich, the mystic saw how our Lady was rapt in ecstasy at about 11 o'clock on Christmas Eve, and how she arose to a kneeling position and folded her hands across her breast. Joseph, who arose shortly after the Blessed Mother, put straw in a manger for the newborn Child. The manger was approximately three feet long, larger than some of the other cribs in the stable. Mary put the Infant in the manger, having covered Him with a long-sleeved shirt and wrapped Him in swaddling clothes. She covered Him with one of the woolen cloths she and Joseph had brought with them from Nazareth. Then Mary and Joseph prayed, she at the left and he at the right of the Child. Joseph raised his hands to the level of his chin, his fingers intertwined, and Mary crossed her arms over her breast. The skies became clear and starlit at the moment Jesus was born.

From the Consecration to the Communion of the Midnight Mass of 1927 Therese saw the glorified Christ Child, though she was at home and abed because of the extreme weakness following Passion ecstasies. She became ecstatic now when the church bells were heard announcing the Consecration. The infant Saviour as she saw Him measured about 40 centimeters and was dressed in a shirt of dazzling whiteness. He stood on a bright cloud and held out His arms and smiled. His hair was fair and curly, his eyes deeply blue: an apparition of more than earthly loveliness. In the distance there was wondrously sweet music.

At 1:20 on Christmas morning, Therese had another vision. She saw a hut built among the rocky hills about a half hour's walk from the stable in which Christ was born. There were eight shepherds in the hut, lying on pallets of rushes, and with them were thirteen favorite sheep, and also one large and one small dog. Near by were seven folds sheltering some five hundred sheep. Suddenly there was a blinding brightness and the shepherds jumped up, frightened. Fearfully they peeped from the hut to see what had happened. They saw an angel in the form of a youth standing on a cloud and wearing a dazzling garment. His left hand was on his breast and his right hand was lifted upward. He had no wings. The whole vicinity was lighted up by the effulgence that streamed from the angel. Then the angel spoke to the shepherds in their language, re-assuringly, with solemn friendliness, while his right arm pointed to Bethlehem. When he stopped speaking he was instantly surrounded by many other angels, about six hundred of them, Resl estimated. All of these angels were radiant forms on bright clouds. They sang a song at least six times to the accompaniment of string and wind instruments, and then vanished. For a quarter of an hour the sheep watchers discussed the matter, after which they prepared to go to Bethlehem, followed by their thirteen favorite sheep and two dogs.

The adoration of the shepherds, the subject of masterpieces of art, was seen by Therese Neumann immediately following the angels' apparition and song. The oldest of the eight shepherds knocked on the door of the stable. Joseph opened the door and they told him what had happened. He said something to them and then pointed to the Child and His mother. He led them to the manger and they looked at the Infant with obvious love and joy. They spoke to the mother, who unwrapped her Babe somewhat, to the amazement and enthusiasm of the eight men, particularly the oldest among them. All of them knelt around the manger and prayed. Our Lady, whose hands were again crossed over her breast, wore a reddish-brown girdled garment, a yellowish woolen veil, large shoulder cloth of wool, and leather sandals. Joseph, whose clasped hands were held at chin's level, wore a dark-yellow, belted garment. The dark hair of his head was uncovered and fell in some disorder to his shoulders. His beard was of middle length, thick and undivided and somewhat lighter than the hair of his head. His expression was composed, mild, friendly. Some of the shepherds wore garments reaching to the ankles or below the knees, others wore the skins of animals belted around their waists. The oldest of them prayed with arms raised up, the others held their hands like Joseph did. All of them were very devout. Their sheep and dogs mingled with them as they adored the newborn Saviour. They gave the Holy Family one of their sheep, but Mary and Joseph soon afterward gave it to a very poor shepherd. A ewe with her lamb which the shepherds later gave Joseph and Mary were sold by them to buy things they needed.

The coming of the Magi and the slaughter of the Innocents at Herod's command were also seen by Therese in Christmas-time visions after 1926 and 1927. In the state of exalted rest she declared that the names Gaspar, Melchior, and Balthasar were approximately correct for the Three Kings. They were really ruling princes, very rich, not ambitious for power, mild and generous toward their peoples. Balthasar came from Nubia, a land with much gold, was in the early forties, and journeyed with about seventy servants, twenty soldiers, eight learned men, and one woman. Melchior came from Arabia, a land rich in fruit and grain, was in the middle fifties and his servants numbered forty, his soldiers fifty, his sages five. He was accompanied by two women. Gaspar traveled from the lands of the Medes, noted for its rosin, incense, and fruit. He was about 45 years of age and had with him twenty servants, forty soldiers, and four sages.

In the three lands from which the Magi came, especially in Media, the study of the heavens was fostered. High wooden towers were built from which to observe the stars, and the princes had court astronomers. Jews of the diaspora, who often lived to be 200 years old, brought a knowledge of the true God and of the promised Messias to them, in particular the prophecy of Balaam: "A star shall arise out of Jacob. . . ." In Nubia the star was seen at least three weeks before the birth of Christ by two magi, who told their king. They said the star was of extraordinary size and brilliance and had a peculiar "tail," long and curved at the end. The king sent news of the star to his friend, Melchior, in Arabia, and he, in turn, notified Gaspar of Media. Having made up their minds to follow the star, the kings started out from their respective realms, met in Media, and continued the journey together. Sometimes the star could not be seen for weeks, even months, and this delayed the royal seekers and their retinues.

It seems that Therese's first vision of the Magi ended abruptly without showing their arrival in Bethlehem. But on the Feast of Three Kings, January 6, 1929, she saw how they reached Jerusalem. The king from Nubia was black, he from Arabia brown, and the one from Media yellow. After inquiring at the court of King Herod, they traveled onward, the star leading them to a stone house outside the city where the Holy Family was staying at the time. They worshiped the Christ Child and brought Him gifts, and at their request His mother placed the Infant in their arms. Finally the Blessed Virgin led the Child, who could now walk, from the stable to where the retinues of the kings awaited them, and all greeted Him ardently and gave Him gifts. The kings were monotheists, knew the prophecy of Balaam, and believed that this was the star of which he spoke.

From the customary long sleep following the Friday ordeal, Therese woke on Easter Sunday to see in five pictures the resurrection of the Lord and the incidents connected therewith in the place of burial, Mary Magdalen and the three women at the grave, Peter and John at the grave, and the Saviour's appearance to Mary Magdalen and to the other women. In the evening she saw the divine Redeemer as He appeared to ten Apostles and showed them His wounds, ate in their presence, and instituted the sacrament of penance. Regarding the Resurrection, she declared that she saw the place in which they had put His body, and all at once Jesus was alive and an angel removed the stone that closed the tomb. There was a frightful tremor, the guards fell down, excepting the one who had pierced the side of the Saviour on the cross. He trembled but did not fall. The wounds in the hands and feet and side of the Crucified had healed and now they were radiant with light. She declared that He was not a form of light but was in the flesh.

While in the state of prepossession after the ecstatic vision, Resl told how she had found herself with a large crowd of people on the way to a mount. All were barefooted and the Lord walked, did not "float" over the earth. His clothes were whiter than snow and the wounds luminous. Then the Saviour swept upward, became smaller and smaller, at last no bigger than a little child, and at last clouds shut Him from sight. His mother was there.

Besides those mentioned, the Christocentric visions granted Therese have included that of All Saints' Day, when she saw the Saviour with angels and saints; His circumcision according to the ancient ritual of Israel; and His baptism by St. John the Baptist. She also had visions of the Blessed Virgin and of several other saints. Not with the elaborate background of Renaissance artists, but rather like primitive pictures are the visions of the Annunciation, on March 25.

According to Resl's statement in the state of exalted rest after a vision, Mary remained in Jerusalem with John for some years after her divine Son's ascension, and then went to Ephesus. About three quarters of a year before her death our Lady expressed the desire to go to Jerusalem, to see once more the places sanctified by the presence of Jesus. They lived in apartments next to the Upper Room. By a more than human intuition, the Apostles gathered in Jerusalem and so were present at Mary's death; all but James the Greater, who had died, and Thomas, who had not yet arrived. On a Saturday they were with Christ's mother and spoke of the Saviour. Mary's yearning for Him became so intense that she swooned in the arms of John and died in A.D. 49. The Beloved Disciple closed her eyes, then kissed the forehead, the right cheek, and the mouth of the Blessed Virgin, as did also the other Apostles.

While the body of the mother of Jesus was being prepared for burial, Peter and James the Less went to see about the tomb in which her body was to be placed that day. Early on Sunday the Archangel Gabriel and Mary's guardian angel came and bore her body to heaven, where she was greeted and welcomed by Christ and the entire heavenly court. The soul of our Lady had been reunited with her glorified and transfigured body. Thomas came to Jerusalem on Monday, and on Tuesday the grave was to be opened. Again, Thomas was late. The Apostles found nothing but the cloths in which the body had been wrapped. Thomas was not satisfied with their explanation, so the tomb was visited once more. From it came such an odor of sweetness that even the Doubter was convinced that the body of Mary no less than her soul was in heaven.

Because St. Thérèse of Lisieux played an early and important part in the mystical experiences of Therese Neumann, it was natural that there should be apparitions of this favorite saint. At first, the Little Flower made her presence known only by the light which Resl saw and the voice which encouraged and counseled the stricken peasant girl. Later, however, the stigmatist was privileged to see the French saint garbed as a Carmelite nun.

Several of the great martyr saints have been the subjects of visions by Therese. The stoning of St. Stephen, the protomartyr, was seen on his feast day, December 26. A trial was held before the high priest, Caiphas, during which Stephen spoke boldly, his face shining with ardor. He then was bound and taken through the streets to a place outside the city walls. For a while he prays standing, while the stones were hurled at him, then he sinks to his knees, and finally to the ground. A ray of light seems to come from his breast and fly upwards. When the light fails, he collapses completely. One word Resl heard him say in his prayers was *Abba*, Father.

Therese saw St. John the Evangelist at the Last Supper. Jesus had said that one of those present would betray Him. Peter spoke to John, demanding that he ask who the betrayer is. John leaned his head on the breast of Christ, and, looking up, asked Him. The Saviour answered sadly. In a later vision, when St. John was older, he wore a beard, which he did not have at the time of Christ's Passion.

Resl saw the death of John at Ephesus, where Mary had been with him from A.D. 37 to 49. After the death of our Lady in Jerusalem John returned to Ephesus, where he died surrounded by a bishop and priests of the primitive Church. His last words were, "Children, love one another."

The martyrdoms of a number of saints were seen on their feast days. St. Catherine of Alexandria (November 25) defended the Christian religion in the presence of Emperor Maximin II and later against fifty learned men, of whom about forty became Christians and were burned to death at the emperor's command. Catherine was scourged and thrown into prison, where angels healed her wounds. The Empress Justina and her retinue and the officer and soldiers who had heard Catherine speak before Maximin visited her in prison and were converted. All were beheaded. Catherine was to be torn on the wheel, but the instrument of torture broke, and she was then beheaded. Two angels bore her body away.

St. Barbara (December 4) flees from a tower when her father becomes enraged at her belief in Christ. She is scourged, burned with torches, her breasts are cut off, and finally her father beheads her. St. Agnes (January 21) refuses the marriage offer of the son of the prefect in Rome, and of the prefect in behalf of his son. She is steadfast when brought before the judgment seat of the prefect, who orders her taken to a house of ill-fame. Her hair grows so swiftly that it covers her body and an angel appears to guard her. The son of the prefect, the only man who dares to approach her, is struck dead. His father at first rebukes Agnes and then implores her, and when she prays the son is restored to life. Later, after being sentenced by another judge, the saint is to be burned at the stake, but the fire does her no harm. Just before her beheading Christ appears to her.

A vision which must have pleased Therese especially was that of St. Francis of Assisi on Monte Alverno when he was stigmatized. Another vision of deep interest was the meeting of St. Peter with our Saviour as Peter flees from Rome to escape the persecution of Nero. Our Lord asks Peter, *"Quo vadis?"* and all the Apostle can say is *"Quo vadis tu, Domine?"* . . . Where are You going, Lord? Jesus tells him He is going to be crucified for him, whereupon Peter returns to Rome. In a later vision Resl saw how Peter and Paul defy Nero and then die, the former crucified head down, the latter beheaded.

CHAPTER 12: A Chapter of Marvels

Each of the mystical phenomena of Konnersreuth is a *gratia gratis data,* a gift of grace freely given by God to one whom He chooses to favor and who responds with heroic selflessness to the promptings of His spirit. In addition to the awe-inspiring gifts of stigmatization, abstention from all food, ecstasies and visions and ecstatic Holy Communion, Therese also has received such other gifts as these: being able to be in two places at the same time, seeing her guardian angel and those of others, seeing into the past and into the future, knowing what takes place at a distance, and being the instrument of cures.

Ritter von Lama declared that to his knowledge the phenomenon of bilocation occurred in the life of Therese Neumann for the first time in December, 1930. In the beginning, there was not a proper appreciation of Resl's apparent simultaneous, visible presence in two places at the same time. It was presumed that the presence of her guardian angel was involved. But later, based on the exact knowledge shown by Therese in her replies to questions, there seemed no longer any reason to doubt that bilocation actually took place.

Early in December, 1930, Father Naber celebrated Mass in one of the churches of Berlin. When he returned to Konnersreuth Therese told him that she had been present in the Berlin church when he celebrated Mass and distributed Holy Communion. As he expressed doubt, she proceeded to recall to him his difficulty in unlocking the tabernacle door and getting a second key from the sacristan. She described the interior of the church and the altar exactly, and all the while she had been physically present in her native village.

Since then the mystic has been able to assist at divine services in the Konnersreuth church while lying bedridden in her room. She has heard the sermons (which she repeated correctly afterward) and mentioned the names of children who misbehaved in church. It was supposed at first that Therese's presence in the other place was purely spiritual. Father Ingbert Naab, a Capuchin, asked her prayers in behalf of the spiritual exercises he was about to conduct for young people in the Palatinate. One day during the retreat he saw Therese for three quarters of an hour while he celebrated Mass and delivered the sermon. He saw her standing in the rear of the church, in her customary black dress and white headcloth. At the same time she was in the home of Professor Wutz in Eichstätt, but had remembered her promise to pray for the success of the exercises. In this instance, however, it was stated, when Resl was in the condition called exalted rest, that her guardian angel had represented her at the retreat.

One evening in the autumn of 1931 a priest of the Diocese of Münster in Westphalia was praying fervently for his sister, a religious in charge of a large charitable institution. Sister F. was sorely tried by misfortunes affecting her loved ones. Her priest brother asked Therese's intercessory prayers, so that his sister's sorrow would serve to advance her spiritual welfare. When Father E. visited Sister F. shortly afterward she told him she had seen Therese Neumann. When he said, "In a dream, I suppose, while sleeping," she answered: "As certainly as I am speaking to you now, I was awake when she appeared to me. It was about 11 o'clock at night and I was in bed, when she came and consoled me." She described the stigmatist: "She was very kind and told me, too, that my brother the priest wished to go to Konnersreuth, and said. 'Tell him to come.' " While praying so ardently for his sister that evening in 1931, Father E. had made up his mind to go to Therese's village. It was the hour at which Resl appeared to Sister F.

A priest who had labored until recently in the Diocese of Campinas in South America has related how, one night as he tossed restlessly on his bed in the mission, Therese Neumann entered the room and asked him: "Reverend Father, will you not share my suffering?" He was utterly amazed and withheld his consent, whereupon Therese disappeared through the door by which she had come. When this missioner came to Europe later he felt himself drawn to Konnersreuth. When he saw Therese for the first time he recognized her at once, for she was exactly as she had been the night she appeared to him in South America. She knew all about the occurrence and consoled the priest because of his refusal to share in her suffering; a refusal, she said, which came from nature's reluctance to endure pain, as with our Lord in the Garden.

An instance which has been extensively investigated by ecclesiastical authorities concerns a chauffeur in Zwiefalten who had crushed a heel in an accident. An X-ray examination revealed splintered bones, and the verdict was that the foot would have to be amputated. The man pictured himself jobless and crippled for life. In their distress, his wife decided to write and tell her troubles at once to Therese Neumann. Hurriedly she wrote a letter, took it to the nearest mailbox, and then stopped into a church for brief but ardent prayers. The second night thereafter the wife saw Therese, recognizable because of her black gown and white headcloth, as she entered the room, approached the beds, and touched the injured foot of the sleeping chauffeur. Then she prayed and vanished from the woman's sight.

The wife of the injured man did not know what to do. Ought she to awaken him and ask whether he, too, had seen the stigmatist of Konnersreuth? She decided to wait until morning. The chauffeur awoke after a sleep untroubled by the usual moanings. He said that he felt no pain, but they decided not to take off the bandages until the physician arrived. When the doctor unbandaged the injured foot he said it was completely healed. Further examination showed that the shattered heel was now in a perfectly normal and healthy condition. The wife told, then, of her letter to Therese Neumann and of what had occurred the previous night. The doctor "withdrew from the case, fearing probably that, if he were to bear witness to an undeniable miracle, he would incur the scorn of some of his colleagues and of a certain clique of scientists."

The days following the end of July, 1934, brought an

important addition to the series of occurrences, says Herr von Lama: "One of my brothers, who is a priest, had been given charge by Therese in Konnersreuth of another priest, a foreigner, and had accepted the task. What this man revealed to my brother enabled him to realize the stranger's perilous situation and, shortly after they had left Konnersreuth together, the latter fell into what was unmistakably a condition of complete demoniacal possession. Each time this happened, my brother was able to gain mastery over the unfortunate man without employing extraordinary means. In dangerous moments, when resistance came in the street or in a railway station, Therese Neumann showed herself to the possessed one and the result was exceedingly effective. This occurred five times during the exorcism which took place with episcopal permission in the rectory at P. Instantly upon the appearance of the sufferer of Konnersreuth, as the demons called her, their resistance broke down.

"It had been Therese who, on a Friday after her ecstatic suffering and in a state of prepossession, had directed that my brother be found at once and sent to the man in question. He had been present during the forenoon at the Passion ecstasy, had been vehemently moved at the sight of the stigmatist's agony, and had left the room as in flight. She continued to show a keen interest in the welfare of the unfortunate priest. The case has not yet (1935) come to an end."[1]

In the state of prepossession, Therese is not only aware of the nearness of her guardian angel, but also notices a form of light at the right of each bystander. Once she

[1] Lama, Friedrich Ritter von, *Therese of Konnersreuth*, pp. 130, 131.

said: "Over there is one whom I can touch," and added in her dialect that he spoke High German. One who marveled how she could, in this state of childlike simplicity, give such astonishingly complete and correct answers to difficult questions, was told by her that it was the voice of her angel guardian, who instructs in a moment. It is sometimes almost impossible to tell whether the cause of her heightened intelligence is a gift of grace or merely an instruction by the angel. Perhaps at times the two are combined.

Therese calls an angel a *"lichta Moa,"* a bright man, for she always sees the angelic presences as forms clothed in an effulgence. The light in which she sees Christ is infinitely brighter than that surrounding the angels; and the souls in purgatory are seen in much dimmer light, varying almost to a dull gray, according to the progress of their purgation. In general, the light in which her visions are flooded is different from the light of the sun, she has said, and in contrast to it daylight on earth is meager, almost a darkness.

The stigmatist's use of Aramaic, the language spoken in Palestine when Jesus lived on earth, is a very interesting phase of this gift of hers. But when the occasion arises she speaks and understands other languages heard in her visions. Thus, when a bishop and his companions on a visit to Konnersreuth spoke Portuguese, Resl realized that this tongue was used by St. Anthony of Padua, a native of Portugal, when the Christ Child appeared to him, as she saw in a vision. She distinguishes between Latin and Greek and between dialects of these languages. In her vision of St. Lawrence's martyrdom, she noticed that the

Latin he spoke was different from that of the judge who
sentenced him. "During a vision of which Smyrna was the
locale, she said that the people there spoke a more pleasing
language than did those in Jerusalem, thus showing a
preference for the superior beauties of the Greek tongue."

In the vision of the Immaculate Conception, the words
of the Blessed Virgin to St. Bernadette are heard not in
Latin, nor in literary French or Spanish, but in the dialect
of the Pyrenees, where the apparitions of Lourdes took
place. Our Lady said: *"Je suis la Conceptiune immac-
ulada."* ... I am the Immaculate Conception. Father Naber
was unable to explain this, but while reading a book about
Lourdes he learned that the words were in a form of
speech prevalent in Southern France. The book gave the
sentence exactly as Therese had heard it.

Linguists have taken notice of Resl's use of Aramaic.
Dr. C. Wessely, the Vienna orientalist and papyrus expert,
spoke of it at a meeting of the Leogesellschaft in the
Austrian capital. He told how Dr. Gerlich, Dr. Wutz, and
Dr. Johannes Bauer, professor of Semitic philology at
the University of Halle, had observed and studied, each
independently of the others, all the Aramaic material fur-
nished by the stigmatist. The New Testament, composed
in Greek, transmits only about sixteen Aramaic words,
and even those in their adapted Grecian forms. Except
for this, then, almost nothing was known of the language
which was the customary one of Jesus and His neighbors;
it was not Hebrew, as many have supposed. Dr. Wessely
says: "It is a matter, doubtless, of correct Aramaic, as it
was probably spoken in Christ's time. That fact of it being
Aramaic is proved. From the grammatical viewpoint,

Therese Neumann's utterances are correct without exception, and they withstand in a noteworthy manner even the strictest tests as to details."

Still another gift bestowed upon Therese is that of discerning relics. She is able to tell, instantly, whether a relic is genuine or spurious, no matter what tests are applied or how firmly the authenticity of a supposed relic may have been held. She can also tell whether a relic is of the first class: a part of the body of the saint; or only a minor relic: a piece of the saint's clothing or something that has touched a relic. Therese possesses this remarkable ability while in either the state of exalted rest or in that of prepossession. Naturally, her whole life being centered in the dear Saviour, she reacts with a special vehemence to the presence or touch of particles from the wood which Jesus carried to Calvary and on which He died.

A Benedictine monk had inherited from his grandmother a supposedly true relic of the cross, which had belonged to nuns who fled from the Rhineland before the Napoleonic invasion. After a Passion ecstasy, the monk put the relic near one of Resl's stigmata. At once she raised her wounded hand as a sign that the particle was genuine, and added that it was from that part of the cross under the Redeemer's feet. The monk also was told that another relic was of a "holy pope and martyr." The label bore the word *linus,* but she did not see this. St. Linus was the first successor of St. Peter as pope and died in A.D. 78.

Dr. Gerlich wrote that on one occasion Father Naber submitted a number of enclosed relics which Therese, without opening her eyes, described as particles of the true cross ("This is of the Saviour's true cross") and gave exact details as to the parts from which they were. (In some instances, "This is of . . . but it has merely been touched to the cross.")

Brother C. submitted the crucifix hanging from the cord of his habit. Therese said: "Genuine and spurious. . . . You believed that there was a relic of St. Francis in it. It is not a true one, but you may continue to reverence it, for it touched a true relic. The one of St. Clare is genuine." When the crucifix was opened, the contents bore two inscriptions, S. Franciscus, S. Clara. She verified the relics of St. Odilo, who died more than one thousand years ago; of Duns Scotus and St. Cecilia, "the maiden whose neck they cut"; St. Stephen, the protomartyr; St. Lawrence and St. Elizabeth. When she identified the relic of Saint Nicholas von der Flüe, who died in 1487, she said: "Oh, my, that was a good man, for he loved the Saviour very much. And do you know, he ate nothing, just as I do. But he had it much better than I, for he was in the woods and the 'shining man' (her designation for the guardian angel) brought him our Lord." Someone asked how often this happened, and she answered, "Many times."

A native of her own village figured in one of Therese's identifications of relics. "This saint," she said, "entered heaven without going through purgatory. He was born in Konnersreuth, then he went to Abyssinia, where he was martyred. One ought to pray for his speedy beatification." She referred to Father Liberatus Weiss, a Franciscan missionary who was stoned to death on March 3, 1716.

The priestly blessing exerts a visible effect upon Therese, particularly when she is in one of her several modes of ecstasy. A priest who witnessed a Passion ecstasy on Friday, December 21, 1928, saw how Resl lay pale, blood-stained, and exhausted by physical pain and mental anguish. Father Naber, deeply moved, spoke to her with a sympathy so intense that no father at the deathbed of his child could have been more solicitous. After several moments of severe pain, her heart grew lighter and she felt a lessening of pain. Father Naber asked her the cause of this, and she told him that the Saviour "did something good for me." This is her customary expression when she receives the blessing of a priest. Father Naber asked if any priest present had blessed Therese, and Father M. of H. nodded. He had given the sufferer his blessing without any of the other spectators being aware of it.

Bishop Waitz of Feldkirch tells in his pamphlet on Konnersreuth how the stigmatist in her Friday ecstasies "feels the whole bitterness of the ordeal, and while she otherwise shows complete readiness to suffer, in this special state she sometimes murmurs, 'I cannot!' or, 'I do not wish to!' It is the revulsion, the horror of nature face to face with pain, as the Saviour Himself knew it in the Garden of Gethsemani when He prayed 'Father, let this chalice pass from Me!' But as soon as she is blessed, Therese gathers herself together again and says, 'Now the Saviour has given me something good. He is so kind!' and joyfully resumes her burden of suffering. When I realized this, I blessed her repeatedly during the course of the forenoon, when she fell into the difficult state and sighed and groaned. And each time I observed what a benefit the blessing was. Never have I seen the power of priestly blessing demonstrated so vividly as during those hours at Konnersreuth."

Therese reacts to blessings not given her in her presence, as for example when Father Naber is in the neighboring town of Waldsassen. She also benefited by the Holy Father's blessing bestowed upon her in Rome. In March, 1930, she wrote down the date on which she had received "something especially good," and soon afterward she learned that a cardinal in Rome had sent her a special blessing on that day, and at about the same time the Pope again sent her his blessing.

As Resl reacts to the spiritual help of a priest's blessing, so she also feels the presence of fallen-away priests. Several of them visited her in Konnersreuth and were mercilessly exposed, but in other cases of sinners there was never an exposure and public humiliation. One of these former priests, who represented himself as an artist, was forced to listen to a litany of his transgressions. "It almost toppled him over," reported Father Naber, who was present.

Dr. Hynek, the Bohemian physician who was a free-thinker until his conversion to the Catholic faith as a result of his Konnersreuth experiences, tells the following incident in his book on Therese Neumann: "A well-dressed man of the upper classes presented himself to Father Naber as a physician and asked permission to examine Therese's stigmata. The permission was given gladly and the pastor conducted the stranger to the stigmatist, who took off her left half-glove and gave the 'doctor' her hand. Suddenly she put her right hand on his shoulder and spoke calmly to him: 'Oh, Reverend Sir, what have you done?' The 'physician' turned pale, then fiery red, and left the room without a word. . . . Later it was learned that he was an apostate priest."

Countless are the appeals received by Therese Neumann, and many cures are attributed to her intercession, as in the case of the chauffeur in Zwiefalten. Willing as she is to help others, though it means suffering for her, the stigmatist is saddened by the fact that so many ask for physical cures. She, who is the exemplar of a heroic attitude toward pain, who through her example teaches submission to the will of God in suffering as in all else, is asked to intercede for others that they may escape suffering. But she has an abundance of human sympathy, and so she prays for those known to her and for strangers, storming heaven for them. Sometimes the Saviour deigns to hear her petition and to effect a cure. However, the number of physical healings is small in comparison to the much more important cures in the spiritual sphere.

There is the case of a woman whose faith in God and in His Church had been imperiled by a grave misfortune. This was followed by the death of her mother, her last moral support. The mother died without the least intimation of her daughter's spiritual condition. In hours of despair, when disgust with life assailed her, the poor daughter would cry out: "Mother, help me! If there is a God, an eternity, you still exist! Oh, help me, help me to regain my faith! Do not permit me to be lost. Pray for me, hear me, mother!" Then one day it seemed to this woman that she heard a voice saying: "You will find your faith again; something is going to happen to restore your faith!" This brought a surcease of anguish, but then her father died, and the daughter was plunged into new suffering and want. Horrible thoughts of suicide tortured her, and there was no one in whom she could confide. In the midst of all these troubles, the woman heard of Konnersreuth. Was this the promised sign?

The afflicted woman decided to go to Therese's village. However, the required episcopal permit was refused, and the former despair came upon her once more and she collapsed. For long months she was bedridden and, according to the medical verdict, her condition was hopeless. Then she heard that the sufferer of Konnersreuth had helped others through letters, and she resolved to write and beg for Therese's prayers and help. After the letter had been sent, the woman wept continuously, was in a turmoil, with only one clear thought: "Therese Neumann, help me! Obtain for me the grace of faith and of a happy death." Her restlessness decreased and she began to pray to the Most Sacred Heart, hesitatingly, like a lost child seeking a return to its Father's house. But these were days of desperate depression and hopelessness. As the weeks passed her physical condition grew steadily worse, until she was convinced that she would live only a few weeks.

Suddenly, close upon a spell of complete dejection, the afflicted woman felt a new sense of restfulness and even of joy, such as she had not experienced for years. She could pray heartily now and her physical suffering abated. Contrary to all expectations and to the amazement of all who knew her, her condition improved. After a few weeks she was healthier than she had been for years, and there was an even greater interior change. She regained her faith in the Real Presence in the Blessed Sacrament, and at the same time felt a deep yearning to join Therese

Neumann in receiving Holy Communion. But to go to confession demanded a heroic conquest of self — a spiritual sacrifice. She visited Konnersreuth in spirit and dwelt in her mind on all that had happened there, on the heroic sacrifice of the stigmatist (which no one would make if there was no God, no Rewarder), and on what had happened in her case.

The following year, healed in body and soul, she was able to go to Konnersreuth, about which she wrote: "Thank God, I found what I had hoped to find, and far more. Not only a strengthening and confirming of my faith, but a great love for the Saviour and the desire, the intense yearning never to grieve Him again, but to love Him always more and more. At sight of the suffering — I was present at the vision of Christ being lifted on the cross — a tremendous change took place within me. I cannot describe what happened. I wept uninterruptedly for an hour, wept as never before. With God's grace I have since then endured all the temptations and hardships of my life with strong courage — I can never thank God enough for the great, the sacred things He has permitted me to experience."

In Voorburg, Netherlands, a man whose initials were J. J. B. worried about his wife, whose condition was so hopeless that death was expected at any moment. She had undergone an operation, and every possible means to help her was used, but all seemed in vain. The husband had shortly before read a book about Therese Neumann by Monsignor De Hovre, so he resolved to write and ask the stigmatist's help. He mailed the letter on October 5. On October 26 a sudden change come over the patient.

She told her husband that the evening before and through-out the night she had been constantly occupied with Therese Neumann, as far as her condition made this possible. Shortly before midnight she was awakened, abruptly and completely, felt a severe pain, then had the sensation of new life flowing into her body. In a short time she was able to travel to Konnersreuth. The husband wrote he was convinced "that in this matter there was supernatural aid."

ALL the titles to which she has a right — stigmatist, faster, ecstatic, sufferer, seeress — may be summed up by calling Therese Neumann a mystic. For the phenomena of Konnersreuth are the fruit of Christian mysticism, the purpose and goal of which is union with God.

In general, mysticism implies a relation to and an initiation into something exceptional, occult, exalted, secret. In philosophy it is studied as the religious yearning of the human soul to be intimately united with the divine; and the system or discipline which tries to effect this union. In Catholic theology it treats of the spiritual acts and states which cannot be achieved by human efforts, not even with the ordinary help of divine grace; and of extraordinary forms of contemplation, visions, and private revelations, and the object of all these, the mystical union.

The writers on Christian mysticism point out that union with God is the fruit of His grace and the reward of all who merit heaven. In the present life it is attained only by a few to whom God deigns to give the special graces that are necessary. Such souls are the mystics in the history of the Church — the chosen men and women who are spiritual mountaineers — while the bulk of Christians are mediocre plainsmen or are content to live in the valleys.

There are Franciscan qualities in the character of Therese Neumann, and a biographer has written thus of the Little Poor Man on the eve of Monte Alverno: "Those close to Francis saw with awed wonderment how he was climbing the third of the three high and mystical stairs by which the soul attains to union with her divine Bridegroom. They knew that Francis had long ago ascended the stair of purgation, at each step of which the soul is cleansed more and more of the stain of sin and the dust of earth; and the second stair, too, had been mounted by this simplehearted man, who knew none of the subtleties of theology, who suspected learning, whose only book was the New Testament with its picture of Christ crucified; the steps of the illuminative way, in which the soul delights in contemplating God and His perfections and in practicing all virtues in a humble imitation of her All-Perfect Exemplar.

"They knew full well that he had also endured the dark night of the soul, when all light and consolation are withheld, when the soul trembles on the brink of despair, clings desperately to the hem of God's garment. And now — now they saw him set his eager feet on the first step of the third stair, the one that ends in the anteroom of paradise, that brings to the soul her ultimate joy on earth, union with God."

One who has studied the phenomena of Konnersreuth might well see Therese's sickness through seven long years and her heroic acceptance of suffering as steps upon the first stair. The ascent is exceedingly painful, for it involves extraordinary physical and spiritual ordeals, but it brings to the soul, also, such extraordinary grace as enables her to bear the agonies and, purging herself more and more of earthly dross and moral imperfections, makes herself worthy of still further graces of an exceptional kind. The process is called passive purification, to show that the graces bestowed are by no means merited by anything the soul might do. However, this does not exclude an active co-operation of the mystic in the work of divine grace.

During her illnesses in young womanhood Resl felt a strong inclination to use her suffering as a soul-cleansing means. At first she asked occasionally that the pain might be lessened. Later she became reconciled to it and offered it as a sacrifice of love, atonement, and intercession. In Christian mystics the passive purification of a soul is always accompanied by a purification of the senses. The intense spiritual suffering is intended to make the soul more and more conformable to her divine Model, as far as this is possible. There are no consolations, no encouragements: it is the Dark Night of the Soul spoken of by St. John of the Cross. It removes the last obstacles, opens the door of the soul to the high grace which will strengthen her for the ascent of the second and third stairs.

A considerable time after the appearance of the stigmata, a visitor in Konnersreuth noticed that Therese was still subject to occasional purgations of the spirit, and he considers this a sign of genuine mysticism, in which the purgative process never disappears entirely, for the whole earthly life of the mystic is a continuous striving toward the sublimest height. Nor was Resl spared the ordeal of temptation by demons while the process lasted. She heard a voice in excellent High German urge her to beg for a lessening of her pain: "Your suffering is senseless. Do you not see that you need only say when you are tortured, 'I will not!' Go to church and be like other people. Do not be fooled, He suffered enough for you." The impression upon her was at times so strong that she was severely tempted. The words, however, betrayed their evil source, especially when there were such sudden exclamations as: "The One-Who-Was-Nailed never suffered. He made believe He did so the people would come to Him. Ha, I have the most of them anyhow."

The best-armed and most valorous soldier is sent to the place of gravest danger in battle, and souls endowed with the highest graces are exposed to the attacks of the fallen angels. No matter how high he has climbed, every mystic is to the end of his life in peril of succumbing to temptation, a Konnersreuth observer reminds us, and adds that for this reason it is an act of charity to pray for the perseverance of such a one.

On the second stair, the illuminative way, the chosen one is suddenly filled with further extraordinary grace, without any action on its part. Therese Neumann shows this in the inward conversations she experiences and also in the visions which present the content of Christian teaching in the most vivid manner possible. The illuminative way is one of progress in the knowledge of divine truths, and Resl deepens her understanding year by year through the visions which repeat themselves but never grow tiresome, and by means of their almost overwhelming themes and realism help her to achieve the purpose of these experiences: to grow constantly in the knowledge and love of God. This distinguishes true from false mysticism, in which frivolity, inquisitiveness, and a seeking after magical secrets play so large a part and so often fill the soul with darkness and pride, instead of producing enlightenment and the humility of genuine mystics.

The third stair, the way of union, is the goal of those who have climbed the first and second stairs. As every Christian is called to the ordinary paths of purgation and illumination, so all are called to an ordinary way of union, through the virtues of faith, hope, and charity, the sacraments of the Church, and the gifts of the Holy Ghost. But there is an extraordinary way of union for mystics. These chosen souls show forth the wholly unmerited graces which God wills to give them; they strengthen the virtues in other souls in an exceptional way. There is granted them the gift of contemplation, an illumination far greater than the light of faith, yet on the other hand far inferior to the light of glory which the blessed possess in heaven.

This mystic contemplation, an extraordinary experience of the divine, forms the essence of Christian mysticism, says a student of Konnersreuth. It is not confined to the intellect but flows into the will, in which it enkindles a heavenly flame of love. The will thus burning with love endows the intellect with an ever greater knowledge of God. Therefore, says Father Fahsel, the essence of mysticism embraces three elements: The gift of wisdom enables the intellect to contemplate the divine; this experience evokes a vehement love on the part of the will; and the love thus engendered leads to the highest form of contemplation. The process is intensified by exceptional gifts of grace, and in its highest manifestation approaches the beatific vision, which the soul cannot attain on earth excepting fleetingly. It seems to him that Therese Neumann possessed the gift of contemplation since her youth. No one can achieve it, no matter how loyally he co-operates with God's grace, unless he is called to be a mystic.

For the will of the mystic, the unitive way means ecstasy. When the power of love becomes superhumanly, almost unbearably intense, the soul thus drunken with love seems to almost separate itself from the body and the senses no longer react to outward stimuli. The body appears dead, although there is no death. The intellect is drawn from the contemplation of its natural objects to the enraptured contemplation of divine things. And the mystic annihilation of self means that the ecstatic soul in its union with God forgets itself and all created things — sees, hears, considers nothing but the Object of its love.

All the qualities, all the experiences, and all the manifestations of mysticism in Therese Neumann's life have caused competent observers to believe that she is indeed a genuine mystic, one who lives in an intimate and continuing union of love with Jesus.

Students of the Konnersreuth phenomena have observed and commented on Therese Neumann's inspirations, and the extraordinary interior directions and impulses which form such an interesting aspect of her mystical state. Often the inspirations come when she is not in an ecstasy, and they come with absolute abruptness. She may be conversing with visitors when, suddenly, she will seem to be listening to a voice at her side. Then, as if responding to something told her, she will make an astonishing announcement or answer an unasked question to one of those present. The inward words are always distinct to her, impress themselves very strongly upon her, with an urgency which is reflected in what she said on one occasion, after she had listened and complied with a command: "I simply had to say that!" She shows a remarkable spiritual certainty in all she says and her demeanor shows that she listens with reverence and that the interior voice instructs her in an instant. She also retains what she hears and repeats it after a considerable lapse of time so precisely that no deviation from the first, original form can be discovered.

There are three ways in which these interior words may be perceived by the mystics, according to writers on the subject. They may come from the physical sense of hearing or through the imagination, or may be "heard" only in the mind. In any of these ways God can form the words directly or through the service of His angels.

On July 17, 1931, the stigmatist, pale and worried, told a visitor, Father Holzamer of Jugenheim, that she had at that moment been seized by an inexplicable concern for the Holy Father in Rome. She could not explain the matter, but felt convinced that the Pope must be in grave danger or faced by an unusual difficulty. For this reason she decided to offer up her sufferings the next day, a Friday, with the intention of helping His Holiness. On Friday morning the newspapers told how a bomb had been placed in St. Peter's on the afternoon of July 17. The bomb was found and taken away, but the fact that later it exploded in a field showed what might have happened to Pius XI and to St. Peter's.

Another phase of Therese's mystic condition concerns the gift of contemplation in the exalted degree which is called the prayer of quiet. It is like a background against which are unfolded many aspects of the soul's union with God, expressed mystically in prayer. The prayer of quiet is so-called because during it the powers of the soul are in a passive condition, not as in meditation during which the reason is at work. The soul is completely at rest and yields to the influence of grace, while the imagination is inactive.

Archbishop Teodorowicz describes how this mystical power isolates the soul, which waits upon the Teacher and Master whom Christ promised and of whom it was said that He would teach all things. He is the pedagogue in Christ, the Comforter, the Holy Ghost. "His interior words, with which He directly influences the power and ability of the soul, are more powerful than the most eloquent spoken words. He meets the soul with overwhelming strength, generally of a sudden, unexpectedly. Hence in the Gospel the Saviour compares Him to the wind which comes we know not whence. . . . Entirely apart from extraordinary mystical experiences, the soul becomes the more passive the stronger the influence of the Holy Ghost that brings the soul into immediate contact and communion with God."[1]

One of the writers on Konnersreuth draws our attention to the fact that Therese Neumann's mystical life and experiences began only after her stigmatization. However, all the announcements of what was to come preceded the

[1] Teodorowicz, Josef, *Mystical Phenomena in the Life of Theresa Neumann*, trans. by Rudolph Kraus, pp. 160, 161.

bestowal of the wound marks; and she has said that she was not at all aware of the mystical states before her stigmatization. Only after she had been stigmatized did they become a part of her life. Her spiritual director did not consider her condition, when she was the victim of stubborn, prolonged sicknesses and suffering, as part of the mystical state. He saw in her an example of the good Christian who submits patiently to God's will. There was no indication of mysticism and she knew nothing about the extraordinary graces that would soon be granted her, nor of the extraordinary events of which she would become the center.

An observer found that Therese's prayer and whole inner life as a mystic has two sides. One is the childlike, simple, loving, happy attitude toward the Saviour, as shown in her conversations with Him and her sayings about Him. The other side is the eloquent silence of her soul — a silence that fills her sleepless nights without tiring monotony. St. John of the Cross declared that the way in which these mystical experiences play their part in the soul of a chosen one is mysterious indeed and hidden: "Neither the soul nor anyone else knows this, not even the evil spirit has any knowledge of it; because the Teacher who instructs is Himself present, where neither the evil spirit nor the natural sense perceptions nor reason can penetrate."[2]

Some of the stigmatist's supernatural conceptions and declarations show what extraordinary illumination is granted to her. This is particularly true of those which involve the gifts of the Holy Ghost, wisdom and know-

[2] St. John of the Cross, *Ascent of Mount Carmel*, Book III, Chap. 14.

ledge. She treats obtuse, difficult, complicated, and exalted matters in a manner which is at once childlike in the simplicity of expression and amazingly mature of content, definition, and solution. She analyzes the deep problem of suffering with an astounding clarity and completely in accord with theological science. A non-Christian received this answer to his question as to the meaning of suffering: "Formerly mankind did not have such a need. Things would be better if men would praise God more. Even a little flower can give us occasion to thank God and to praise Him. The Saviour permits suffering to punish certain sins, to test the fidelity of those who love Him, and to give men an opportunity to help others. These sufferings are never so great that a person cannot bear them or must be unhappy, if he has the Saviour within him."

A priest tells how he and a learned Dominican began to discuss the question of faith and grace in Resl's presence. They talked learnedly, quoted St. Thomas Aquinas, but the stigmatist said: "Why do you say it in such a complicated way?" and proceeded to answer the question so wonderfully, with such profundity and clarity that tears began to well up in the eyes of the Dominican, who said afterward: "How ingenuous and simple that was! Yet never have I learned so much dogmatic and pastoral theology in so short a time."

Father Fahsel, in his book on Konnersreuth, declares that the great Christian mystics differ from ordinary and far lesser people chiefly in this, that in their phenomena there are occasional qualities and states which belong to the paradise of the past and to the paradise of the future.

In the first paradise, man lived in a mystical union with God, and there was no care or sorrow, neither sin nor sickness nor death. But the blessedness of the second, the final paradise, is even greater. Eden meant a time of probation and a Godward development of man. The heavenly paradise means that man has attained the promised bliss, in which his soul is united with God in the light of glory. The spirit participates in the highest manner in the knowledge of God, the human will is completely merged in the divine will, and the resurrected body partakes of the celestial light in such a way that it is no longer an instrument of the soul's Godward evolution but is the material, outward reflection of all the happiness which the soul now possesses.

The lives of the Christian mystics, says this author, remind us particularly of qualities and states which Holy Writ and the Doctors of the Church attribute to the coming paradise. The mystical phenomena in the life of Therese Neumann recall for us, he declares, the Bible's and the Church Fathers' descriptions. At times her soul seems to belong to another world, and though even the brightest illumination of the highest contemplation on earth is far from being the light of glory in heaven, yet it seems to be in some measure a reflection, a foretaste of that celestial brightness. In her contemplation, ecstasies, and visions, her use of the gifts of wisdom, knowledge, discernment of spirits and of things, prophecy and healing, "the soul of Therese Neumann already takes part to some extent in the condition of the soul in the paradise that is to come."

To this chronicler as well as to many others, Therese Neumann the mystic seems to be a living bridge spanning the world in which we live with the world announced by Jesus in the Gospels and believed in by His Church.

W HAT manner of child and girl was this mystic of Konnersreuth, and what manner of woman is she about whom are centered all these amazing phenomena? What sort of village is Konnersreuth, which has become so irrevocably linked with the name of Therese Neumann, as other towns have become forever associated with one man or one woman who lived there — Assisi, Lourdes, Siena, Bois d'Haine, Ávila, Lisieux?

Therese Neumann was born in Konnersreuth on Good Friday, April 8, 1898. Her mother asserts that she was born shortly before midnight, but the vital records of Konnersreuth report the birth as having taken place on April 9, 1898, at 1 a.m. According to the baptismal record in the parish church Therese was born at 12:15 a.m. on April 9 and christened on April 10. A declaration by Resl while in the state of exalted rest seems to settle the matter. She confirmed her mother's statement as to the day and the hour of her birth.

Eleven children were born to Therese's parents, Ferdinand Neumann and Anna Grillmeier. Therese was the eldest. The others and the years of their births are as follows: Maria Anna, 1899; Anna, 1900; Engelbert, who died young, 1901; Otillie, 1902; Engelbert, 1904; Crescentia (Zenzl), 1906; Augustine, 1907; Agnes, 1909; Ferdinand, 1911; and John, 1912. All of the children were born in Konnersreuth and baptized in the village church, which is dedicated to St. Lawrence, whose martyrdom Resl has seen in visions on his feast day, August 10. Her father is also a native of Konnersreuth, where he was born June 16, 1873. He has been described as of the Alpine type, rather tall and slender, with pronounced features and black hair, now gray. Her mother, the daughter of a farmer, was born at near-by Neudorf, in Konnersreuth parish, on October 23, 1874. She is considerably smaller in stature, her face broader and less sharply featured. Later in life she became quite stout and her brown hair became gray. Both parents are strong, well into their sixties and seventies, and have seldom been sick.

The whole world knows her as Therese Neumann, but in her native village, where she spent her entire life, she was at first known as *die Schneiderixenresl*. It is a Bavarian custom to call people by the names of their homes rather than by that of the family. The grandfather of Ferdinand Neumann, Resl's great-grandfather, was a tailor named Felix Neumann. From his being a tailor, *Schneider*, and his Christian name being Felix, the people coined the name *Schneiderix* for him and *Schneiderixenhaus* for his home. In 1868 the house burned down, and because he had to borrow money to build a new home he was forced to be content with a smaller building, the one-story, peak-gabled cottage in which all of the Neumann children were born. In 1917, when Therese was 19, the house was enlarged by building a gable at the front to add second-story rooms.

Not much is told us about Resl's childhood. She had some of the minor sicknesses common to children, but had never been seriously sick before March 10, 1918. At the age of three she went to live for a while with Therese Forster, her godmother, whose Christian name she was given in honor of the great Spanish mystic, St. Teresa of Ávila. Frau Forster was Resl's aunt, her father's sister, and lived in Waldsassen.

Father Witt tells of this period of Therese's life that she was a well-behaved, lively, and attractive child. There is extant a photograph of her when she was about three years old. At Christmas time while at the Forster home Resl received her first doll and she was immensely delighted with it. But after a few days the novelty wore off, and she discovered that the fair playmate had sawdust "insides" and cared no more about the doll, because, as she explained, "it had no life in it." Nor did she care to play with her sisters' dolls. To the regret of Herr and Frau Forster, who were childless, Resl's parents soon took her back home, as they could not bear to be separated from her.

The mystic of Konnersreuth grew up in poverty; not sordid destitution, but poverty grim enough. When Ferdinand Neumann inherited his Grandfather Felix's trade and his cottage, the home was heavily mortgaged. It required the hard, ceaseless work both of him and his wife to meet the mortgage payments and care for their rapidly growing family. He toiled at his tailor's bench and sewing machine, and helped his wife as much as possible work the small piece of land attached to the home. They had four cows, and raised potatoes, a staple of the family diet, and the other crops usual in their district. There were no luxuries of any kind in the humble home, only the barest necessities. A few incidents will show that if the wolf never actually got into the house, he was at times near enough to show his teeth.

When Therese had grown old enough to go into domestic service on a neighboring farm, she noticed how butter was used generously in the more prosperous household. Telling her mother of this, she was told that such use of butter was usual but that the Neumanns could not afford it. She was admonished not to say anything about this to her mistress, because otherwise her parents would feel shamed.

When Tailor Neumann had finished a suit, the children delivered the garments to the customer and would sometimes receive a few small coins for this service. Instead of spending the money for candy or other objects of childish desire, the coins were regularly and joyfully deposited in a drawer of Herr Neumann's sewing machine. Then, as happened more than once, if the time came when there was no money in the household purse, the family would gather around the sewing machine, the drawer would be solemnly opened, and its contents of some 30 or 40 *Pfennigs* used for what was most urgently needed. The little ones were proudly happy to help in this way.

Resl remembered one occasion when there was no money in the house. It was the anniversary of the village church's dedication, always observed with religious solemnity and with something special at the principal meal in even the humblest homes. Herr Neumann had finished a coat for a rich farmer and he hoped the payment would enable him and his wife to provide a little something more than the year-in-year-out meager diet of their children. But the rich farmer did not even mention the matter of payment and, lest he offend this customer, the village tailor said nothing, but returned home silent and downcast. However, Frau Neumann managed somehow — as mothers so often manage — to supply something that added a bit of festive touch to the everyday fare.

Despite the poverty and hardships of their early years, Therese and her brothers and sisters grew up healthy and strong. Such was the spirit of co-operation in the family, such the sturdy resignation and the training in going without things that Resl looked back upon this period as a happy one. Family affection cast its genial glow over what might otherwise have been a drab existence — family affection and the discipline and strength which the strict Christian atmosphere of the home engendered.

Herr and Frau Neumann have always been not only practical but ardent Catholics, and they saw to it that each child was trained as early as possible to follow in their footsteps along the religious path. Obedience was insisted upon, but there was also careful impartiality. No child was favored above the others. The parents tried to keep their sons and daughters under their supervision as much as possible, discouraging visits to the homes of playmates and running in the streets of the village. Generally, a severe glance by the father was enough to correct the boy or girl inclined to be spunky or disobedient. When necessary, they were spanked. Herr Neumann was especially insistent upon good behavior in church. If any of his children failed in this regard, the culprit was sentenced upon returning home to kneel on boards that were anything but soft and pray an entire rosary.

Little Therese accommodated herself readily, happily to the strict regime of her home. She did not find poverty irksome, and when she began to go to school she adapted herself to the new life with characteristic thoroughness, energy, and cheerfulness. She entered the village school on May 1, 1904, at the age of six, and left it May 1, 1911, at the age of 13. The parents encouraged their children to do their "homework" faithfully and Herr Neumann liked to review the lessons with them in the evening while he was busy at his tailoring. Resl's teacher testified that she was an excellent pupil in the subjects of religion and handiwork, and good in reading, composition, arithmetic, and penmanship. After finishing the village school course, Therese went to Sunday school for three years, from May, 1911, to May, 1914. She was much interested in the catechism lessons, and after discontinuing Sunday school she studied this manual of Christian doctrine at home. The notebooks in which she wrote her catechism lessons were destroyed when the addition to her parents' house was built in 1927.

Strict as the discipline was in the Neumann household, there was never anything puritanically excessive or morbid about it, but a strong sense of Christian duty and no less of Catholic optimism. Resl received her First Holy Communion on April 18, 1909, at the age of 11. She showed nothing beyond the devotion of a normally pious Catholic girl of her age. She was healthy, strong, devoted to her parents and brothers and sisters, and eager to help. Being the eldest of the children, she soon learned to care for the younger ones and to help her mother as much as possible. Perhaps because of her early disappointment with her doll while at her godmother's home in Waldsassen, she preferred picture books, and even more the cultivation of plants. She began her childish horticultural attempts by knocking the handles from some of her mother's cups, so they would look more like flowerpots. Of course, she had to find other vessels in which to put her plants.

Work in the home pleased her, especially when it meant helping her mother, who had to spend some time in farm work. Resl scrubbed the floors, dusted the rooms, and did the washing. She delighted in doing this work in her mother's absence, then gleefully showing her the whole wash on the line when Frau Neumann returned from her labor in the field. Nor was she above bragging a bit to her mother about the work she had done, as she has smilingly admitted.

Dr. Gerlich points out a significant aspect of Therese Neumann's character in her formative years. She did not like fairy tales, stories of magic, or exaggerated legends. Once when her father read a fairy tale to her, she objected strenuously that such a story could not possibly be true. Already in her first year at school she was displeased when the teacher related fairy tales, because to her they were so obviously false. She never indulged in daydreaming, read no romantic fiction, and legends of the saints did not appeal to her. On the other hand, she enjoyed hearing true stories and biographies. She partook generously of the solid, nourishing, and not at all sugary mental fare of books on the Catholic faith, the Gospels, and Epistles. Later, when she had become a domestic servant, she read a magazine called *Notburga,* issued especially for hired girls, and another magazine, *Rosenhain,* the purpose of which was to foster devotion to St. Thérèse, the Little Flower of Jesus. And she read a German version of St. Francis de Sales's *Introduction to a Devout Life.* Her love of flowers made her an eager reader of books and magazines on horticulture.

The economic situation made it necessary for the Neumann children to add what they could to the family income as soon as possible. During the last half year at the village school Resl began to work at 1 o'clock in the afternoon on an estate called Schloss Fockenfeld, about a 15-minute walk from Konnersreuth. Long afterward she recalled how happy she was when she could give her father the wages — about 15 cents — she earned for each half day's work. When she was 14 years old, in 1912, she went to work for Max Neumann, the owner of the largest estate in the village. He owned a large house, a tavern, bowling alleys, a stable housing 16 or 17 heads of cattle, and large fields beyond the town. Max Neumann was no relative of the Ferdinand Neumanns. Resl's parents were glad that she, and shortly afterward their next eldest daughter, Maria Anna, found work in the village, for that enabled them to keep the girls under supervision.

The people for whom Therese worked maintained a Christian household, but it was difficult to satisfy their demands. The work was heavy, particularly after World War I broke out and the retired owner's son, Martin, and the male servant were called into military service in 1916.

The strong, healthy daughter of Ferdinand and Anna Neumann did not shrink from any task given to her. She was able to do the work ordinarily left to men. She plowed, operated a planting machine, and in February, 1917, was put in charge of the farm's oxen.

Dr. Gerlich says Therese told him she had always preferred and enjoyed men's work to women's. She had learned to sew and knit, but took no interest in needlework, crocheting, or embroidery. She would rather wash and clean than cook. She liked it best when there was plenty of work, so that one had to "take hold with both hands," and especially if the weather was good she delighted to work in the field. She preferred to work out of doors, for then she had adventures that she cherished. In winter, when snow lay deep in the pine forests of the region, deer would emerge to seek food. Wood hens and rabbits would come to her with complete trust and let her feed them.

Therese worked chiefly in the fields and cattle barns, helping in the tavern only during meetings or dances. Once in a while she drank a little beer, when the day was hot and the work hard. She never danced, though she had to serve beer to the dancers. However, she was no spoilsport, and was glad to indulge in any decent merriment. Eventually another sister, Anna, joined her and Maria Anna at the Max Neumann establishment, and naturally Resl oriented and instructed her younger sisters. Her sturdiness of character and her energetic, almost masculine qualities fitted her splendidly for this task.

She made use of these qualities, too, in another matter. She found favor in the eyes of some of the young men, but the feelings were not mutual. She refused to consider any suitor because she had chosen her vocation — she wished to join a community of Sisters with missions in Africa. Once she leaped down from a considerable height to escape from a scamp who became too bold. Another young man, persisting despite her repeated declarations of not being interested, finally succeeded in forcing her to accept an invitation to an evening tryst. Resl prepared for the occasion by taking along the end of a whip, and when the fellow appeared she plied him with such vehemence that he ran to escape the blows and never bothered her again.

Slowly, by saving a part of her wages, she accumulated enough for the dowry which she would need upon entering the convent, but the war prevented her entrance. Her father had meanwhile been called into the army, and her mother, because the family needed her earnings, asked that she wait until the war's end. Resl agreed, at the same time making the firm resolve that she would no longer be kept from her desire once the conflict had ceased.

Thus Therese Neumann lived and worked in the fields just outside of Konnersreuth or in the village which was soon to be so intimately associated with her name. Konnersreuth is a market town of about 1400 people, in the eastern part of Bavaria, close to the Czechoslovakian boundary. In the center of the village is the customary square, an open space dominated by the Church of St. Lawrence, a Baroque structure with the bulb-shaped steeple common in that section of Europe. Near the church, which is surrounded by a large, walled garden, is the home of the pastor, Father Naber. Also fronting the square are a number of houses, the majority of them only one story high, and in one of these was born and now lives the stigmatist, the seeress of Konnersreuth. The houses cluster too closely together to allow for gardens or trees, but there are blooming plants in almost all the windows.

Of the thousands who have visited Therese Neumann's village, one of the most recent was Father Speer Strahan, an American army chaplain. He tells how, turning from the highway at Waldsassen, he struck out over the open fields, passing on the right a dark forest in which Nazi snipers had concealed themselves to fire upon Americans until their ammunition was exhausted, and then came out to surrender.

"Next, the outskirts of the little farming village, whose blackened walls and charred open space made one wonder how so small a village could produce so many ruins. Then the central square of the village, which was neither a square, nor yet a circle, nor even a pentagon, but a combination of all three, with an inn on one side, a fountain in the center, to the right the yellow-walled house of the Neumann family itself, and opposite a village church rather larger than one had thought to see here, with a flight of stone steps up to it, and above the curious onion-shaped dome that becomes increasingly common as one travels across Thuringia and Bavaria to the east." The church, "even amid the debris and the discouragement of war" was "as exquisitely clean as a nuns' chapel, with all in a restrained good taste, including a handsome new side-altar with a bas-relief of St. Thérèse of Lisieux in glory, surrounded by roses."

Flaxen-haired children lead the chaplain and his G.I. clerk to the rectory. "There was a few minutes' wait in the bare uncarpeted little parlor, then steps could be heard on the stairway, and in a moment an elderly priest was shaking hands with us. It took one no more than an instant to see that we were in the presence of an extraordinary man, who was now smiling in kindly fashion behind his steel-rimmed glasses, while his simple and elegant Latin revealed a man of eminent common sense and a theologian. Later one learned that Father Naber was even then celebrating his fiftieth year as a priest, that he had come to Konnersreuth when Teresa Neumann was ten years old. One did not, of course, need to be told that he would die there."[1]

Father Naber told the American chaplain that up to that time about 12,000 American soldiers had visited the village, to meet and talk with and ask the prayers of Therese of Konnersreuth.

[1] *The Ave Maria*, Nov. 16, 1946, p. 615.

CHAPTER 15: A Time of Dolors

On SUNDAY, March 10, 1918, Therese got up a little after 5 o'clock and hurried to finish her early chores in time to be at church for the 7:30 o'clock Mass, at which she intended to receive Holy Communion. She finished the work in the cattle barn at about 7 o'clock and was returning to the house when Christian Sölch, a neighbor, called attention to smoke rising in the air over the stable of another neighbor named Schmied. Curiosity and also concern because the stable was close to her parents' house caused Resl to hurry home. She awoke her father and told him there was a fire at Schmied's. Then she ran to the fire and joined the men in doing what could be done, leading a calf and a pig out of the burning stable and taking them to the near-by inn of the *Weissen Ross* (White Horse) for safekeeping.

She noticed how people were running toward her employer's buildings, and when she got there saw that the Max Neumann property was threatened because the wind was carrying sparks and blazing straw to the wooden roofs and walls. Resl thought of her belongings in the upper story of the house, so she hurried to get them and carried them to a neighboring house. They included her best clothes, among them her Sunday dress. Then, hurrying again, she joined the other servants and the neighbors who were fighting to save the endangered buildings. It was her suggestion that someone stand on the roof of the shed at which the flames were now lapping and that buckets of water be handed up to him to keep the wood moist and in this way perhaps prevent the fire from spreading. Accepting her proposal, the proprietor himself went to the roof, and because she was so strong, Resl was chosen to lift the pails of water from a stool up to him on the roof. She took the pails filled with water in her right hand, and with her left hand she supported and pushed them high over her head. The pails weighed from 20 to 30 pounds, and because some of the water always spilled, she was soon drenched. The work was so strenuous and her employer found it so exhausting that he urged Resl to lift the pailfuls of water higher, but she replied that she was doing all she possibly could. After more than two hours of this labor, and just as she was about to lift another pailful of water as high as she could, she felt a sudden, sharp pain in the small of her back. The pail fell from her grasp and her right foot slid from the stool, but she prevented falling to the ground by clinging to the wall. Two of those who were carrying water ran to help her, a woman of the neighborhood and a gypsy girl. However, Resl was able to get off the stool without their assistance. She could walk around, but she could no longer lift the pails of water.

The accident took place at about noon, and soon afterward Therese noticed that her feet "felt queer"; or rather, that they felt numb, as though they were asleep. She found it impossible to climb the stairs to her room to change her drenched clothing, so she went to the stable to feed the cattle which had been neglected because of the fire. She could neither bend nor lift, so she decided to eat something (having fasted because she had intended to go to Holy Communion that morning), and go home, for she wanted to lie down and rest. The pain in her back gradually became worse and spread throughout her body. Walking home was very painful, and she had to drag herself along, bent forward. To her mother's anxious question she answered that she had hurt her back so that it felt as though someone had tied a rope too tightly around her waist, and that there seemed to be a numbness in her lower body. Toward evening she felt less exhausted, but the pain had not lessened. Nevertheless she returned to her room in her employer's home, managing to climb the stairs only by holding on to the banister with one hand and raising herself at each step with the other hand.

Despite the constant pain, she tried to work, for male help was scarce due to the war and she felt she was needed. Her fellow workers resented the loss of her strength and her employer spoke unkindly to her. She remained at her employer's home, doing what she could. Early in April, some weeks after the fire, she suffered another serious accident, falling down a stairs and striking her head against the stone step at the bottom. She was taken to her own home, where signs of bowel and bladder trouble soon became evident, a source of extreme embarrassment to Resl. A painful cough, first noticed after the fire, clung on stubbornly. The pain in her back was especially excruciating when she put her hands to her back in dressing.

Thus the young woman who had been so merry, so warm-hearted, who had delighted in hard work, became somewhat morose. It was decided to take her to the hospital in Waldsassen.

Therese Neumann entered the hospital on April 23, 1918, at the direction of Dr. Goebel. Dr. Seidl, in charge of the hospital, was serving as army surgeon. There was some lessening of the pain in the small of the back and of the inclination to vomit, but on the other hand the convulsions which had begun to assail her before now became more severe. One of these seizures was so bad that the hospital Sisters said afterward they thought Resl would die. The patient did not like the methods of Dr. Goebel. She suffered hunger, the prescribed diet being very meager, and the prolonged idleness became so unbearable that she thought of leaving the hospital secretly, but the Sisters hid her clothes.

Finally, at her request, Dr. Goebel released Therese on June 10, 1918. She remained in his care so that she could continue to get the sick insurance benefit to which she was entitled. Resl tried to make herself useful around the home, though her condition was substantially the same as before. She fell while working in a shed, convulsions seized her and she became unconscious, awakening to find herself surrounded by a crowd of gaping children. Her mother, back from the fields, carried her into the house and to the bed, where she was to remain for two or three weeks. At that time as at the first accident on March 10 of that year. Therese suffered severe pain in her head and eyes. Now, after the fall early in August, eye trouble set in. When she wished to read to relieve the tediousness of being bedridden, she had difficulty in doing so, especially because her prayer book was in small type.

Once more, recovered somewhat, Resl tried to make herself useful, but collapsed in the cellar of her home. Again and again she was seized by cramps, which caused excruciating pain in the small of the back, whence it spread to her legs and feet, arms and hands, and particularly to her neck and the back of her head. Her mother sent her to another physician, Dr. Wilhelm Burkhardt, who lived in Hohenberg an der Eger but had regular office hours in near-by Arzberg. Kind people in the village gave Resl a ride all or at least part of the way from Konnersreuth to Arzberg and back for the consultations, for in her condition she could not possibly walk the distance. She liked Dr. Burkhardt, whom she remembers as "a good, lovable, old man."

It seems that during one of Dr. Burkhardt's examinations of her, Therese felt for the first time how serious her condition was, and how hopeless the outlook. Years later she said to Fritz Gerlich: "Think of it, *Herr Doktor,* a young person looking forward with joy to the vocation he has found! I wanted to be a Mission Sister, and I never imagined it would be otherwise! I would have managed it, too, don't you think so? And then . . ." tears came into her eyes at the memory of that sad hour.

On October 19, 1918, Resl went to her former employer's estate, where there was more than the usual activity because the next day was *Kirchweihtag,* the festival celebrating the anniversary of the village church's dedication or consecration. While working in the vegetable cellar she fell and struck the back of her head. She remained there unconscious for about an hour when her sisters found her and managed to carry her to bed. The former pain in her head was much worse now and her eyes pained her, too. It seemed to her that they were trying to tear themselves out of their sockets. After a few hours her sisters were able to take her home and put her to bed.

The next day, Sunday, she felt so miserable that she thought the end was near, but so much did she desire to go to Sunday Mass and to confession and Communion, that she summoned every bit of remaining strength and managed somehow to reach the church. While still in bed she had tried to use her prayer book, to prepare for reception of the sacraments, but she could not see the book clearly and the pages were no more than a jumble of black on white. Nor could she recognize the people in the street. To herself she said: "Be careful not to let mother know, she'd worry so! This will pass away." She was able to reach the confessional, her pew, and later the Communion railing only because the way was so familiar to her. Before the Mass was ended she had to be taken home and put to bed again. Because she hoped that ardent prayers would help, she insisted upon being taken to the church for evening devotions, and once more she had to be brought back home before the services were over. She could see less than in the morning. The next morning she was able to tell darkness from light, but no more. Early on the morning of October 22 Therese collapsed, and so critical was her condition that Father Naber was summoned and he administered the last sacraments. The priest's white surplice and that of the acolyte with him was all she could see.

Herr Neumann was with the army at Liege, and because of the situation at home, the mayor of Konnersreuth sought an emergency furlough for him. The mother and all of the children excepting one daughter, Crescentia, were ill with the grippe; and Resl, also believed a victim of the epidemic, seemed near to death. When her father came home she could not see him as he stood beside her bed. He saw not the merry, vigorous, busy daughter to whom he had said good-by upon entering the army, but a thin, pale, bedridden young woman who suffered constant pain and whose sight was failing. Her condition was plainly worse than when he saw her in the Waldsassen hospital when home on an earlier, brief furlough.

The grippe epidemic having abated, Dr. Goebel was once more able to visit Resl. He found that there was something the matter with her heart, in addition to all else, and prescribed digitalis. Convulsions continued, some of them so sudden and strong that she was thrown from her bed. Another accident happened about the middle of January. While playing with her youngest brother, Hans, she fell out of bed and injured herself. She was unconscious for some days and suffered repeated convulsive seizures, but said nothing of the cause to her parents, lest her little brother be punished. She liked to have him and another small brother in her room, for they made the monotonous days more endurable. Her father and mother and older brothers and sisters did all they could to relieve the tedium of the days and nights as much as possible. But they had their work, always pressing, so Resl was largely dependent upon her brothers Hans and Ferdinand, about 7 and 8 years old, for companionship.

After his discharge from the army, Herr Neumann saw Dr. Seidl of Waldsassen crossing the village square. He knew the physician, who had shortly before returned from army service, and asked if he would take charge of Therese. The doctor prescribed medicine for her stomach, and for what was apparently a new affliction, gallstone trouble.

March, 1919, began with some improvement in Resl's condition; at least she believed so. Dr. Seidl visited her twice in the middle of the month, and Resl can remember that then she was not yet completely blind. Dr. Gerlich believes that she lost her sight entirely on March 17. While her mother was changing her bed, Therese fell from a chair and struck her head against the casing of the kitchen door and then against the kitchen's stone floor. She was seized with cramps and became unconscious. She remained thus for a number of days, suffering especially in the head and neck and eyes. She kept her eyes closed and recognized no one excepting her mother among those who came into the room or approached her. Her hearing was impaired to such an extent that she could hear only shouted words, and those very indistinctly. Nor could she speak.

So that they could the better attend to her, Resl's parents had moved her bed to a first-story room. It was now necessary to remove her to the second floor, because customers of her father and other visitors were sometimes witnesses of her convulsions and expressed horror at what they saw. In her second-story room the invalid used a stick or cane to pound on the floor beside her bed in order to summon help. Her condition was so critical during this time that one night Father Naber stayed at her bedside until two o'clock. One day, after having kept her eyes closed since the accident of March 17, she opened them and thought it was night. She heard her parents speaking in the room, and said: "Mother, turn on the light!" Frau Neumann answered that it was noon of the day and the day bright. But there was darkness for Resl.

Therese's suffering caused additional hardship to the family, and distressed her mother in particular. Often Therese felt warm drops on her right cheek and knew that the poor woman was weeping. Her improvement in hearing and speech was temporary, and, after two more falls, followed by convulsions and still another affliction, ugly bedsores appeared on her body. The first of these appeared during the first third of the year 1919. Dr. Seidl prescribed applications but relief came chiefly from a home remedy, chicken fat, recommended by sympathizing neighbors. Thin membranes formed over the sores, often breaking soon afterward. Some of the sores healed, but new ones soon formed on other parts of her body. At times, there were as many as five, six, or seven sores from her shoulder to the base of her spine, and these wounds and the liquid that came from them caused such a disagreeable odor that is was difficult for anyone to stay in her room. All the other ailments remained, too, with only an occasional and temporary improvement. Vomiting followed any attempt to eat solid food, and the coughing up of blood betrayed stomach ulcers. Sores appeared under the left arm, at one time there were eleven of them, the scars of which still remain. Rheumatic pains attacked the patient and there was a swelling of the neck, a paralysis of the swallowing muscles.

This was the pitiful, seemingly hopeless condition of

Therese Neumann seven years after the accident while fighting the fire on March 10, 1918. She was now 27 years of age, bedridden, often for a long time paralized, beset with pain in almost every part of her body, and with almost all bodily functions seriously or to some extent disturbed.

Years afterward Resl spoke with emotion and came near to tears when she told of the long years of invalidism. To one friendly visitor she said: "My God, if I had known all that I would have to suffer, I do not believe I would have had the strength to go on living." She stressed the fact that she had never known illness and had reveled in the hard work her strength allowed her to do, and how the contrast was terrible: from being in perfect health and exceptional vigor to become gravely ill and finally a helpless invalid, chained to her bed for years, as helpless as a baby, unable to help others and completely dependent upon others for help. She felt sorry for her family, particularly for her father and mother to whom Resl's condition was the source of intense parental worry.

Like shafts of sunlight breaking into the gloom of a saddened room was the family affection of the Neumanns during Therese's seven-year ordeal. Resl spoke with moving appreciation of all that her parents and brothers and sisters did for her. They spared no effort or expense within their limited resources to make her lot less painful. There was a loving desire to show her that she was not a burden, chiefly by acting as far as possible as though things were normal, and making her an integral part of the family circle. If Herr Neumann intended to buy a cow, Resl was consulted, as also when the question of what to sow in this field or that one came up for decision. When there was a festival, all gathered in her room. She was the darling of the household, made to feel that she was beloved and her presence and counsel helpful and appreciated. Each night the mother gave her daughter holy water with which to make the Sign of the Cross, and a crucifix, the meaning of which was being made constantly more clear to the bedridden, suffering woman.

CHAPTER 16: Light and Voice

THERESE of Konnersreuth had been devoted to St. Thérèse of Lisieux for years before the accident which began her long ordeal of sickness and blindness. The veneration of the saints had, of course, been a family heritage and custom. In 1914 the father brought home with him two pictures of Sister Thérèse of the Infant Jesus, the French Carmelite nun who had taken so large a part of the world by storm, though she was as yet not canonized nor even beatified. Her pictures appeared everywhere, articles and books about her were numerous, and French soldiers in World War I made her their special patroness.

In sequestered Konnersreuth not much was known of the Little Flower. Herr Neumann, when he was off to war, was given two little pictures of the Carmelite of Lisieux by an acquaintance. As his eldest daughter was named Therese, he imagined that the likeness was of her patron saint, Teresa of Ávila. One report is that he gave Resl one of the pictures, another that she asked him for it. At any rate, having read the text on the reverse side of the picture, Resl found that this was not the great Spanish mystic but a saintly, as yet uncanonized, modern nun.

She liked the friendly face of Thérèse of Lisieux so much that she went to Waldsassen and asked the Franciscan Sisters there (with whom she had been in contact for some time) to tell her more about the Little Flower. They gave her a copy of *The Story of a Soul,* little Thérèse's autobiography, which captivated the larger, far sturdier Therese. Out of her small savings the peasant girl bought other reading matter about the Carmelite of Lisieux, put her picture above her bed, and treasured a relic of her. There was about the Little Flower a spirit of simplicity which attracted Resl, whose native simplicity has always been of the clearest water, neither colored by all that has happened, nor diluted by the passing years.

Therese Neumann followed with lively interest the course of the Little Flower's cause of beatification, and so she was aware that on April 29, 1923, the Church would declare Thérèse of Lisieux a *beata,* enroll her among the blessed, who are generally later canonized and proclaimed saints.

Ferdinand Neumann, early on the morning of April 29, went to his afflicted daughter's bedside to say good-by. He was making a little journey "on my account," as she phrased it. Resl was awake, heard him say, "I am going now," but could not see him. Half an hour afterward, at about 6:30 o'clock, Therese suddenly opened her eyes. She beheld her hands and her white nightgown. She asked herself, "Am I dreaming?" rubbed her eyes, and looked about. "I saw once more the sacred pictures on the walls and greeted them as dear old friends after a long separation." A woman came into the room, but the invalid did not recognize her. " 'Who are you?' I asked, and her answer betrayed her astonishment. Then I knew by her voice that it was my sister Zenzl. During the time that I had been blind, more than four years, she had grown very much. That is why I did not know her."

Frau Neumann was called and Resl cried out to her: *"Mutter, i seh fei!"* . . . Mother, I see well! The poor woman was dumbfounded, perhaps afraid to believe that her daughter's sight had really been restored. She asked Resl whether she was dreaming; then with hands that trembled she held a potted plant before Therese's eyes, and at once the girl stretched out a hand toward the white flowers. Another sister, Otillie, was called, and Resl said: "Why Ottl, how tall you've grown!" The mother held another plant before the eyes of her daughter, who put out a hand again and this time said that the red flowers would be fitting in the church. Hans, the youngest child, was summoned to join in the occasion of joy and thankfulness. He sprang from his bed in his night shirt, and even in such a solemn moment Resl could make a gay remark, playing on the length and whiteness of the little fellow's garment: "Well, Hans, did you come from church? Are you an altar boy?" He, too, brought a flowering plant to his sister as a test of the good news.

The mother and three daughters wept for joy and awaited impatiently the return of their husband and father from Neustadt. He had gone there to get a recipe which had seemed in the past to help Resl when a stomach ulcer burst and she vomited blood. When Therese saw her father that evening, for the first time in four years, she did not mention what she noticed at once, how gray his dark hair had become.

On Monday, Frau Neumann sat beside her daughter and read to her from *Rosenhain*, a favorite of Resl's because it promoted devotion to the Little Flower of Lisieux. The name means "Bower of Roses," in reference to the pledge of the Carmelite that after her death she would let fall a shower of roses upon the earth, in the form of spiritual and material favors. Frau Neumann noticed how Resl, too, read from the magazine and was overjoyed. Here was proof that her daughter really could see again. The girl's sight was restored so completely that she could read even small type, like that in her prayer book.

Dr. Seidl came next day from Waldsassen to call on his patient. He, too, was dumbfounded when Therese told him, "I can see!" and was at first inclined to attribute the restoration of sight to the medicine he had prescribed a few days before. However, when he was informed that the prescription had not been filled until after the cure, he asked Therese what she believed had happened, who had helped her. The mother spoke her mind in answering for Resl: "Yesterday Thérèse of the Infant Jesus was beatified; and she, we believe, helped our Therese." Herr von Lama wrote in 1927 that faith, which the Church approves, may give this explanation, even though there was for the present no compelling reason for accepting a causal connection between the two occurrences. To this he added in parentheses: "Therese, in semiecstatic condition when she told me on August 26, 1927, of her conversation with St. Thérèse, maintained that such a connection existed."

On the back of the little picture which her father had given Resl was a prayer for the beatification of the Little

Flower. Therese recited this prayer every Sunday, and when she learned that the beatification was to take place, she recited the prayer daily and began a novena of prayer for this intention. However, she had not been able to pray on all of the nine days, because of her extreme weakness, so the novena was not completed when Thérèse of Lisieux was enrolled among the Church's blessed. The invalid had not undertaken the novena as a plea for the restoration of her health, because she had by this time achieved a measure of resignation, in contrast to her vehement desire for health at the beginning of her ordeal of sickness. She had asked, however, that she might have the childlike spirit of her beloved little Carmelite; her childlike simplicity and her absolute trust in God. And Resl had need of such absolute trust, for though her sight had been restored and the pain in her head had lessened, the other afflictions remained and new ones were added.

She still could not walk or stand or even sit up and the convulsions and fainting spells continued. In June or July of 1924 an ulcer formed in her throat, which caused excruciating pain and became so large that it was almost impossible for Resl to breathe. On one occasion Father Naber was summoned to bring her the last sacraments because she seemed so near to death. In November of that year a severe cough bothered the invalid, followed by a new ear trouble, which took away her hearing in one ear. A little blood came from her eyes at this time, but her sight was not in the least impaired. While playing with her youngest brother Therese fell from her bed, suffered convulsions, and after she was put to bed again by her sister Maria and had regained consciousness, she felt a severe muscular contraction. Her left leg was drawn up so that it was pressed against the right one. Exceptionally painful heart trouble developed, too.

In this condition, Resl could not lie on her right side because of the crippled left leg, nor on the left side because of her heart. The constant lying in one position led to terrible bedsores on her back and legs. The left foot ulcerated for more than a half year and finally almost all flesh from ankle to toes had disappeared from it. A hospital Sister named Regintrudis contrived "rings" which eased somewhat the pressure of the left foot on the right leg. Dr. Seidl was worried about the situation and in April, 1925, began to fear that the left foot would have to be amputated. The whole family was downhearted at this prospect, and the anguish of her mother hurt Therese Neumann more than all the pain of her afflicted body. "For the sake of her mother, who did not conceal her troubled thoughts, Therese prayed for a slight improvement at least and with confidence in the intercessory power of Sister Thérèse, she permitted three rose leaves, which had been blessed and had been touched to the tomb of the Little Flower, to be placed on the bandage when the wound was dressed. Had not the rose been the favorite flower of the Carmelite of Lisieux? After a few minutes the wound ceased to hurt, and when the dressing was removed it was seen to be closed and covered with a thin, fresh membrane. After a short time, the healing was complete. The rose leaves had been sent to Therese by a Carmelite priest."

On the third Sunday in May, 1925, Blessed Thérèse of Lisieux was proclaimed a saint by Pope Pius XI at a solemn ceremony in St. Peter's. Therese of Konnersreuth was still paralyzed, the spine still as though broken and powerless, so that it could not support the upper body, and while its wound was healed, the left foot was still drawn up under the right leg. For approximately a year and a half the invalid had suffered from ulcers in the head, from which pus issued through the eyes and ears. She had not left her bed of pain since October, 1918, a period of more than six years. Once more, anticipating the canonization, Resl had begun a novena in honor of the Little Flower. She did not ask that her shattered health be restored, because she had surrendered her will to the will of God, having reached this stage of perfection. Father Naber says: "Not until today (May 17, 1925) did she say to me, 'During the past three years I am sure that I have not prayed even one Our Father to get well again.' " And then he goes on to tell what happened on that Sunday:

"Contrary to their custom, Therese's parents had remained at home during the afternoon devotions on this Sunday. During the services in honor of the Queen of May, Therese in her bed prayed the glorious mysteries of the rosary. She had begun to meditate on the second mystery (the Ascension) when, suddenly, there was a bright light about her, as she told us immediately afterward. An electric light, and even the light of the sun, was dim in comparison to this light. She was frightened at first and cried out. This brought her parents to her bedside. Later (which she could not afterward recall) she called out, 'Mother, where is Father Naber?' They called me then and a Mallersdorfer Sister came too. I saw Therese looking steadily at an object toward which her arms were outstretched. Her face beamed with joy, she nodded her head, bowed with exquisite courtesy, and moved her hands as would a lady in waiting who conversed with her gracious princess. Involuntarily I said to the nursing Sister, 'Thus God honors His saints!' All at once Therese sat up, which she had not been able to do for six and one-half years. She had, before my arrival, sat up, but it had caused her excruciating pain.

"After she was again lying down, her face retained the transfigured look. This vanished and she began to weep bitterly because the glorious light was gone and all was drab once more. She grasped for the stick, always at hand, which she used to summon her people. She was, therefore, unaware that we were present. Then I spoke to her: 'Resl, what has happened?' Instead of answering my question she declared with an assurance so absolute that it amazed us: 'I can now sit up!' and did so. 'I can walk, too!' she announced, and then Frau Neumann examined her daughter's feet. The leg which had been drawn up was now in normal position. After a gown had been thrown about her, she began to walk, as yet, out of carefulness, with assistance. Her steps were the first in six and one-half years. I asked again, 'Resl, where have you really been?' And this time she told me (after the others had at her request left the room) with astonishing assurance what had taken place.

"After the wonderful light had appeared, a mild, friendly voice began to speak. She had seen no one. 'Resl, do you wish to get well?' 'I answered,' said Therese, 'it is all the same to me — to get well, or to remain sick, or to die. Whatever the good God wills.' The voice: 'Resl, wouldn't it give you joy if your sufferings were lessened;

if you could at least sit up and walk?' I answered, 'Everything gives me joy that comes from the good God.' The
voice: 'Resl, I shall cause you to have a little joy. You
shall be able to sit up and walk!' 'When I thereupon sat
up, it seemed to me that something took me by the hand
and helped me.' The voice: 'But you shall still have much
to suffer. However, fear not. I have hitherto helped you
and I shall help you in the future.' There is scarcely
anything as painful to Therese as praise. She is fearful lest
the praise bestowed upon her be denied our Lord and
St. Thérèse. . . . The voice spoke particularly of the value
of resignation, humility, and suffering. After it had spoken
this sentence twice, 'It is through suffering that so many
souls are saved,' it concluded, as though wishing to permit
itself to be identified: 'I have already written that far
more by suffering and by persecution than by eloquent
discourses does Jesus wish to build up His kingdom.'
Therese could not remember where these words were
to be found, and was delighted when I showed them
to her. They are in the Little Flower's sixth letter to
missionaries."[1]

The cure of May 17, 1925, included restoration of two
dislocated vertebrae, the vanishing of all evidence of
paralysis and of convulsions, and the disappearance of the
festering bedsores on her back, though the day before they
had stained the fresh bed clothes with blood. Using a
cane, because she was still weak, Resl was able to walk
about. Her parents insisted that she spare herself, so it
was not until June 11 that she went out of doors. Leaning

[1] Von Lama, *Therese Neumann* (Milwaukee: Bruce Publishing Co.,
1929), pp. 23–26.

on her father's arm, she walked across the village square
to the church, to thank God.

Therese herself describes the next marvelous and mysterious happening: "On September 30, 1925, at 12:30 o'clock in the morning, I was still awake and was reading the litany in honor of St. Thérèse by the light of an electric lamp. Nothing could have been more unexpected than what happened. Of a sudden there was a light in front of me, the same light as when I was cured of the paralysis. It came very suddenly, as it had the first time, as suddenly as lightning. In comparison with it, electric light is darkness. . . . I saw and gazed: Light, but no form, no figure. . . . Then I heard a voice, the same voice. . . . It said: 'You can walk now without assistance. The pain that comes from your eyes shall be lessened, but in place of it there shall come intense suffering. . . . Encourage the people to have confidence in God. . . .' 'But,' I interposed, 'I do not myself know whether I am on the right track, or whether I am doing everything in a wrong manner. Some say my case is a fraud; others are angry with me. It is enough to make me doubt whether I am doing everything as it ought to be done. . . .' Thereupon the voice: 'Follow your confessor's counsel in blind obedience and confide all to him. You must free yourself more and more from self. Preserve your childlike simplicity. . . .' The voice ceased and the light disappeared."

The light and the voice gone, Therese stood up and strode about her room for a quarter of an hour without support of any kind. When the church bell rang early in the morning, she walked down the stairs and across the square to the church — the first time in seven years without assistance. September 30, 1925, was the anniversary of the death, and thus of the entering into glory, of St. Thérèse of Lisieux.

The suffering which the voice had said would come did not fail, nor was it long delayed. Resl became bedridden again on November 7, 1925. After enduring the most intense pain for three days she was so weak that she could not even open her eyes. Dr. Seidl, coming in the evening of November 11 in answer to a summons, declared that it was a case of appendicitis and that the patient would have to be taken to the hospital at Waldsassen at once to be operated on. He would not be responsible, he said, if the operation were delayed until the next morning. The distracted parents sent for Father Naber, in the hope that he might advise against taking their daughter to the hospital. But he, after consulting with the physician, who was recognized as an authority on appendicitis, told the parents they ought to consider Dr. Seidl's verdict as the voice of God.

Herr Neumann hurried to arrange for transportation and Frau Neumann feverishly gathered bedding and clothes, but Resl called her parish priest and spiritual adviser to her bedside and asked him if she might not implore little St. Thérèse to help her, so that she would not have to be operated on, if such were the will of God. She told Father Naber that she did not object to the operation, but wished to escape it because her mother was lamenting so inconsolably. When the priest told her it would be all right, she had a relic of the Carmelite saint placed on the sore spot, "and while those present prayed to the Little Flower, the invalid in her bed turned like a worm in agony." She prayed mentally, no more than this: "It is all the same to me, St. Thérèse. You can help me. It is all the same to me, but you hear how mother carries on."

All of a sudden Therese sat up somewhat and opened her eyes. Her face became as transfigured. Her hands were lifted up and stretched forward, and she was heard to say a few times, "Yes." She then sat up, pressed her fingers against the abdomen repeatedly, and said: "Really!" To Father Naber's question, had St. Thérèse perhaps come again and helped her, she answered, "Yes, and she told me I must go to church at once and thank God. Mother, bring me a dress."

The pain and fever were gone. Resl explained that a hand had appeared, and she had wished to grasp it but could not. It was a white and delicate hand, like the little Flower's hand in pictures of her. The first three fingers were outstretched, the others closed. Resl said also that it was the same light and the same voice, and that the voice had said: "Your complete submission and joyous endurance of pain pleases us. That the world may know that there is a Higher Power, you shall not have to be operated on. Arise and go to the church, but at once, and thank the Lord. You shall still suffer very much, but you must not be afraid, not even when the interior suffering comes. It is only in this way that you can co-operate in the saving of souls. But you must die more and more to self. Preserve your childlike simplicity."

Therese's mother objected to her going to church at the time: "Now, at night — it was seven o'clock — out of the heat here, with your fever!" But Father Naber said:

"If St. Thérèse was here to help you, let us go at once, as we are!" A little procession of ten persons crossed the village square that evening, with Therese in the center, and entered the church. During the night that followed the pus passed from the inflamed appendix in the natural way. Early the next morning Resl received Holy Communion, and thereafter journeyed to Waldsassen to report to Dr. Seidl and have the cure recorded.

CHAPTER 17: The Battle

THERESE NEUMANN said
to the voice in the light, at the time of her fourth cure,
on September 30, 1925: "Some say my case is a fraud."

The number of those who said this at that time must
have been small; and small also the number of those who
refused to admit that there was fraud, conscious or
unconscious. The news of Resl's healing had not yet spread
far beyond the village of her birth and near-by places,
such as Waldsassen.

But less than a year afterward the number of those who
took sides had increased tremendously, for in March,
1926, Therese of Konnersreuth had become an ecstatic
and a stigmatist. The cures had been amazing enough.
Here were phenomena even more baffling. So intense was
the interest in the mystic's wounds and fasting, ecstasies
and visions, that very little attention was given to a further
cure, which ended a sickness during which Resl's death
seemed inevitable and near. She arose from what was
thought to be her deathbed and walked to church. To
those who were aware of it, this cure after the beginning
of stigmatization corroborated all that they held concerning the earlier ones.

Believing in the possibility of miracles in the present

no less than in the past and that no other explanation squared with the facts, many found no difficulty in accepting Therese Neumann's cures as supernatural. They pointed out that the ravages on Resl's body proved the reality of the diseases; that physicians had for years exerted themselves in vain to bring about even one cure; that the healings were sudden and the recoveries telescoped into an astonishingly short time what would ordinarily require a lengthy convalescence; and that promises of cures were made by the voice in the light and in each instance the healing followed as promised.

The believers maintained that if natural forces were at work in the Konnersreuth cures, then the natural forces were used by a supernatural power to achieve its purpose, to do what neither science nor nature unaided could do. They referred to the classification of miracles by St. Thomas Aquinas. If two bodies occupied the same space at the same time, or if the sun were turned back in its course, these would be miracles of the first degree. The raising of the dead to life and the giving of sight to the blind are miracles of the second degree. A third degree of miracles consists in this, that the powers of nature are surpassed by the way in which something happens, as when someone is cured of a disease instantly and without treatment or the usual processes of nature. The believers held, too, that the character of Therese Neumann and the characters of her family and Father Naber inspired complete confidence, precluded the possibility of deception.

Father Witt tells us that Dr. Seidl said regretfully to Therese's parents, "I am powerless." The worried mother asked, "What is to become of our Resl?" and the physician answered, "There would have to be a miracle." To an acquaintance who asked about Therese he said: "If she were to be cured there would have to be a miracle."[1] And the voice had told the invalid, on May 17, 1925, at the cure of paralysis: "But you shall be permitted to suffer much more and for a long time, and no physician shall be able to help you." Again, when the acute appendicitis was healed without an operation, on November 13 of that year, the voice disclosed the origin of the cure and the correctness of Dr. Seidl's diagnosis by saying: "That the world may know there is a Higher Power, you shall not have to be operated on."

Some students of the Konnersreuth case were inclined to accept one or more, but not all of the cures as miraculous. A number of these wished to distinguish between sicknesses traceable, as they believed, to the accident at the fire, and sicknesses which in their opinion had no connection with the accident. Archbishop Teodorowicz, in his book on the mystical phenomena in the life of Therese Neumann, asserts that one of the cures "possesses a supernatural character that stands without doubt: the cure of the deep sores." He refers to the bedsores which came from the paralyzed Resl lying so long in the same position, and the sores which developed when the left leg was crippled and forced against the right leg until "the left leg from the ankle to the toes no longer had any skin, the ankle was exposed." It was feared that the left foot would have to be amputated. Instead, there was a cure, sudden and complete.

[1] Witt, Leopold, *Konnersreuth im Lichte der Religion und Wissenschaft*, Vol. I, p. 102.

Other students of the case believe that the cures of
blindness, paralysis, appendicitis, and bronchial catarrh
and pneumonia, no less than that of sores, "possessed a
supernatural character that stands without doubt." On
November 16, 1926, Therese fell seriously ill with bronchial catarrh and pneumonia. The next day she was so
weak that she fainted while going to confession. She had
a high fever, recognized no one about her, and Father
Naber considered her condition so critical that he administered the sacraments of the dying. Resl's face was deathlike in appearance, she almost choked, and her breathing
was so labored and faint that death was expected at any
moment. Then she raised herself up very suddenly,
breathed easier, and sank back onto the pillow. Her
appearance was normal again and her limbs were warm.
Toward morning the pain vanished, she coughed up the
phlegm, and after daybreak was able to walk to church.
At this cure after the stigmatization, as at those before it,
there was the light and the voice speaking from the light.

Among the students of the Konnersreuth phenomena,
some who were honestly skeptical at first became believers
after careful investigations. Others — and for the most part
these did not come to Konnersreuth — kept on insisting
that there were no miraculous cures, that the healings
could be explained naturally, by recourse to one or another psychological process. They spoke and wrote of suggestion, autosuggestion, catalepsy, somnambulism, imagination, hallucination; most of all, hysteria. Suggestion
means a transfer of wills, the imposition of a stronger will
upon a weaker one. There is no evidence that anything
like this happened in the case of Therese Neumann, who

was always strong-willed, clearheaded, inclined to be independent rather than dependent. Autosuggestion means that a person uses his own will to impress the product of his fantasy so powerfully upon his mind that he mistakes the imagined thing for fact and reality and makes it the basis of further action, continued fantasies. But Therese was always sober-minded, rather matter of fact and practical, no dreamer of fanciful daydreams. It will be recalled that even as a child she disliked fairy tales because they were too fantastic for her taste, contrary to the truth to which she was always devoted. They are guilty of fantastic imaginings who try to explain so many diseases which often threatened death, and the cures of them, by recourse to this or that psychological excess or defect.

Indicative of the confusion among the antimiracle writers and speakers, of how they drew contrary conclusions from the same unwarranted premises, was the fact that one group said Therese had a pathological desire to suffer, a martyr complex, while another group said she wished above all else to escape pain, exerted all her will power and every psychological resource to regain her health. At the beginning, some moroseness is recorded on Resl's part. She dreaded the prospect of long invalidism, the trouble she was causing her family, and the shattering of her ardent hope of working for the Negroes in Africa. She told more than one of her friends, in later days, how hard it was for her to be a bedridden invalid. She had all of a normal person's reluctance to be tortured by pain and the perfectly reasonable and natural desire to regain her health and once again be the young woman of exceptional strength she was before the fire.

A study of the facts shows that there was nothing abnormal in Resl's earlier desire to be released from pain, nor in her later willingness to suffer. The one was rooted in her natural human nature: the other sprang from such a heroic, self-sacrificing love of God and man as can begin and continue only when human nature is strengthened and transfigured beyond itself by something more than natural, by divine grace, the *charismata* bestowed upon chosen and responsive souls. For Therese, the cures of her many sicknesses did not mean the end of suffering. She has for twenty years endured the pain of her stigmata, of her ecstatic sharing in the Sacred Passion, and her intercessory ordeals for others.

Even more vehement than the controversy regarding the cures was that which was caused by Therese's stigmata. Because of their sensational character, continued presence, and inescapable implications, the wounds were from the first subjects of defense and attack, belief and denial. The reality of the stigmata could not well be denied, so the battle turned on their origin. The believers declared that this was plainly supernatural, and pointed out that, stupendous as it is, stigmatization is no new thing in the Church's history, but a well-known phenomenon of genuine Christian mysticism. Some of the skeptics came, saw, and believed. The kind of men who diagnosed Resl's sicknesses and pronounced their verdicts from afar stated that her wounds were the result of some sort of trickery or else of disease. It is absurd to say that any but a hopelessly abnormal person and one willing to deceive would, if he could, inflict upon himself, or allow others to inflict upon him wounds which would cause and continue to cause excruciating pain and then pretend that they were divinely bestowed. All the evidence shows that Resl of Konnersreuth never was the victim of any psychological abnormality. It shows also that she has always been scrupulously honest and that she as well as those about her were trustworthy in the highest possible degree. Thousands upon thousands have seen Therese since she became a stigmatist and have seen the stigmata of her hands. Some, including skeptical visitors, have seen the other wounds. Not one has been known to leave the village with the conviction that the wounds were fraudulent. A representative statement is that of Dr. Naegle, a university professor, in the *Deutsche Presse* of Prague, July 25, 1926: "Whoever observes the occurrences at Konnersreuth with unbiased eyes must admit that the stigmatization of Therese Neumann is not a fraud, but a fact which cannot be denied. The wounds are there, they can be seen by all, and they bleed or have bled." Another: "The natural candor of her spirit is probably one reason why, of the many thousands who have been witnesses of the remarkable happenings, not one has dared to say that the girl is guilty of deception."[2]

If the stigmata are of natural origin but not produced by trickery, the only alternative is disease. But there are insurmountable obstacles. In the first place, history knows no case of genuine stigmatization outside of the Catholic Church. Yet there are many non-Catholics of deep spirituality, who strive to please God. Is there then a disease which attacks none but Catholics and which produces stigmatization? If so, all who become stigmatized would

[2] Hollnsteiner, Dr. J., in *Wiener Reichspost*, Dec. 25, 1926.

have to suffer from the same disease, and this has not been true. Therese Neumann suffered from many diseases. Which was the "Catholic" illness which caused the stigmata? And in a number of instances, including that of St. Gemma Galgani, the wounds were bestowed while the recipients enjoyed good health. Some have attempted to establish a causal connection between stigmatization and the cessation of the periods, forgetting that there have been forty-one male stigmatists.

Is it not utterly fantastic, contrary to all common sense, to say that there is a disease which attacks none but Catholics? A disease, moreover, which produces not ordinary wounds but wounds which do not fester and resist all attempts at healing; which appear not haphazardly on the body but only where the divine Redeemer was wounded during His Passion; wounds which are more or less exact reproductions of the Saviour's, and in some cases show even replicas of the nails which pierced the hands of the Crucified; wounds which bleed only on certain days, in harmony with the Church's liturgy?

A pioneer student of the Konnersreuth phenomena who continued his study of them for years, tells us that an examination of the sufferings of the stigmatists (including those which preceded the bestowal of the marks), shows that their maladies were not unknown, mysterious, indefinable ones, but such as constantly assail thousands of their fellow men, "without producing a single stigma in any of these thousands." Therese's sicknesses were such as her physician was well acquainted with, and yet the stigmata appeared! It is to be noted, too, that the preliminary sicknesses are of the most varied kinds. How, then, could they produce in all instances the same effects? How could they cause exactly the same results in exactly the same organs? This contradicts the natural law that similar causes have similar effects. It can be maintained, therefore, that there is no known sickness which produces stigmatization.

Neither deception nor disease being a reasonable explanation, a sensible basis on which to maintain the natural origin of stigmata, there remains nothing but to admit a supernatural origin. And if the wounds are produced by something more than natural, is the power that produces them bad or good? It must be demoniacal or divine. In the case of Therese Neumann there is a simple test, provided by Catholic theology and based on the Church's teaching. Stigmata bestowed by God will reflect Him. The one on whom He bestows them will live in complete submission to His will and to the spiritual authority of His Church. The effect of divinely bestowed stigmata will be to draw the soul constantly closer to God, not farther from Him. The devil tries to make men offend and resist God, to become proud. The high graces which accompany genuine stigmatization generate love of God, an ardent desire to please Him, and a humble and submissive resignation.

A writer on Konnersreuth says that applicable here are the words of our Lord: "I confess to thee, O Father, Lord of heaven and earth, because thou hast hidden these things from the wise and prudent, and hast revealed them to little ones" (Luke 10:21). The life task of the Little Flower was to call attention anew to the "way of spiritual childhood" and to teach others how to walk in it. This is the way

Therese Neumann has walked; to it the voice directs her constantly. But which of the men of science in attempting to explain the "riddle of Konnersreuth" has taken into account the predisposition of Therese Neumann, the atmosphere in which she has lived, and the characteristics which found their fruition in the sacred marks which she bears?

Some excitement was caused, among those interested in the Konnersreuth case, when in 1932 there appeared what was called "a putative Protestant stigmatist." She was declared to be incurably hysteric and when subjected to strong hypnosis and suggestion produced "a flow of blood the size of a pinhead." The "flow of blood" ceased as soon as the hypnosis and suggestion stopped. A materialistic-minded physician who was also a psychiatrist reported that when he wished to examine this alleged stigmatist, together with another doctor, she told him that the "stigmata" were not genuine and that those who believed in her had been duped. It seems that there have been men and women who were able to produce what are called "reddenings" or some sort of bloody sweat. But in all instances they prepared for this by specified psychical manipulations and then managed to produce the bloody spots by nervous or psychic straining; or through hypnosis. All of these "spots" disappeared shortly, and nobody has thus far proved that true stigmatization occurs outside of Catholic mysticism.

"How Science Explains It" was the caption of an article in *The American Weekly* in October, 1939. The author was listed as "Maurice Chideckel, M.D., distinguished American psychiatrist," and what he wrote was part of a general story on Therese Neumann, occasioned by what was said to have been a Budapest dispatch that she was dead.

Dr. Chideckel wrote that "materialists and students of psychology know that there is no supernaturalism in nature and no miracles." He then asked how the phenomena of Konnersreuth could be explained. Dealing chiefly with the stigmata, he said that what the writers of a century ago called "the stigmata of crucifixion" was now known as "autographism and also as dermographism." He said that words, signs, and wheals traced on hysterical persons "are prominently left for a considerable length of time. They may last weeks." In 1939 Resl of Konnersreuth had had her wounds for thirteen years.

This writer declared also that "In religious hysteria it is quite common for a patient repeatedly to make the sign of the cross on any part of her body and sometimes a cross, large and prominent, will appear. Such signs are mostly made on the chest. Due to a congestion of the superficial blood vessels, the rush of blood into them, known as 'hyperemia,' the cross will bleed, sometimes profusely. It is hardly needed to dwell further on the appearance of the cross and the bleeding wounds of Therese Neumann. Dermographism is a sign too well known and too often discussed by dermatologists and psychologists." What was needed was due consideration to the honest, truly scientific reports on the Konnersreuth case, the careful verdicts of competent men who went to Konnersreuth.

Dr. Chideckel did not say how profusely such "crosses" bled; nor how the frequent discussion of dermographism can help to explain stigmata nowhere near the chest. If the profuse bleeding of which he wrote was no more than the "size of a pinhead," or one of the "reddenings" produced by psychic effort or by hypnosis, they were not at all the same as the stigmata of Therese Neumann and cannot be discussed on the same basis. Also, there is no warrant in the literature of the Konnersreuth case to suppose that Resl ever made the Sign of the Cross anywhere or in any way different from the usage of millions of Catholics the world over; or that any "cross" ever appeared on her body. Nor does he explain how genuine stigmata sometimes disappear, returning only during Lent.

After informing his readers that "a part of the human brain does not always function" and in "that part memories, words, and images are stored away that do not come to the fore unless under certain conditions," Dr. Chideckel stated that "Therese Neumann may have heard Hebrew and Latin phrases from the bishop at least once. Many bishops are also great Hebrew scholars. The disturbed cortex of Therese, during an hysterical trance, released those Hebrew words and phrases which she could not utter when the hysterical attack was over."

Not Hebrew and Latin but Aramaic words and phrases aroused the chief scientific interest in this phase of the Konnersreuth case. The words and phrases were such as Resl had no opportunity ever to have heard; such as not even bishops who "are also great Hebrew scholars" would be likely to know, or knowing, use when or where Therese might have heard them.

Dr. Chideckel wrote that "her [Therese's] hysteria caused anorexia, loss of desire for food. While life is impossible without water, one can live many months when just fluid is taken. That she tasted no food at all is doubtful. She probably drank some milk, and milk contains all the constituents needed for the human economy to keep going." He knew nothing about or ignored the fifteen-day strict observation period, the testimony of those on the alert throughout that period, and all that was found and reported regarding Therese's complete abstinence from nourishment. Above all, he ignored the fact that she had lived without earthly food of any kind not "many months" but thirteen years, up to the time he wrote.

The last paragraph in Dr. Chideckel's article read: "Therese most likely died of dehydration, drying up of the tissues, due to slow starvation."[3] Six years after this was written, six after the reputed dispatch announcing her death, Therese Neumann was found in good health by American soldiers and their chaplains and other visitors to Konnersreuth.

The American Weekly containing Dr. Chideckel's scientific explanation contained also an article on Konnersreuth by the Rev. John La Farge, S.J. He wrote that "Therese's character seems to contradict the picture most of us make (and the doctors make) of a woman who has unusual psychic experiences. Jeanne Danemarie, a French woman journalist, visited Therese about 1932, and made a list of the traits that generally accompany abnormal psychology." Women who have the neurosis of hysteria are as a rule variable, restless, taciturn, abulic (unable to make up their minds), suspicious, anxious, emotional, sensitive, dissembling, in a word, abnormal. "But every-

[3] *The American Weekly*, Oct. 15, 1939, pp. 12, 17.

body who has come into close contact with Therese declared her to be the opposite of all these things. . . . Therese, in other words, was no neurotic, and that idea had to be dropped in dealing with her."[4]

One who was known as an opponent of the Konnersreuth phenomena's supernatural origin wrote as follows on the possibility of artificial stigmata: "I, therefore, wish once more to synthesize what led me to believe deception by the stigmatized as out of the question in the case at hand. (1) It was established by microscopic examination that a real flow of blood took place in her case. (2) The spontaneous beginning of the flow of blood was unquestionably observed by a number of physicians, some of whom used a magnifying glass. (3) The quantity of blood is such that it could not very well be brought about by artificial means, without, in such repetitions of bleeding, leaving telltale scars behind (e.g., in the conjunctiva of the eyes). (4) In the heart wound there is not a discharge of pure blood, but a bloody serous flow that could hardly be brought about by artificial wounding. (5) Every tendency to pus is lacking; this could scarcely be avoided in repeated artificial inductions of bleeding. (6) The change of the hand stigmata at the termination of the ecstasy bespeaks a spontaneous somatic change of condition. (7) And it can be added, too, that the supervision of the patient for fourteen days was so thorough as to exclude any likelihood that injuries unnoticed by those ordinarily about her would fail to be observed by experienced persons."[5]

---

[4] *Ibid.*, p. 12.
[5] *Münchener Medizinisches Wochenblatt*, Nov. 18, 1927.

Like her sicknesses and cures and stigmatization, Therese's ecstasies and visions were also proclaimed supernatural by some, and merely natural by others. It was said of her ecstatic visions of the Passion (as it was said of her wounds) that they resulted from an intense, excessive preoccupation with the bitter suffering that preceded and accompanied the death of her Saviour. From childhood to young womanhood, Resl's spiritual life was that usually found in well-behaved, pious but by no means pietistic children and youths in a thoroughly Catholic home and environment. If, as has been reported, she wept with pity when the history of the Passion was read to the children at school, this was no more than many tenderhearted boys and girls have done, none of whom became stigmatists or ecstatics. Her devotion to the Passion of Christ was in concord with her character: robust, deep, and free from any sentimentalism. The Little Flower was Resl's special model, and the Little Flower's way of perfection is that of spiritual childhood, without the least intimation of exceptional, stupendous, or mysterious phenomena. The tailor-farmer's daughter had never read the account of Anna Catherine Emmerich's stigmata and visions, or any other writings of this kind. She was an exemplary Catholic young woman who wished to go to Africa and live out her life in obscurity and hard work as a missionary Sister. She had no other ambition, and there was never anything like exhibitionism in her strong, frank personality. Surprise and misgivings overwhelmed her when she was chosen for mysticism and all its consequences.

Learned men, who know what psychology can and what it cannot do and what part it may have had in Therese

Neumann's case, have testified in the matter. The Archbishop of Lemberg declares that, granting the possibility
of hysterical conditions creeping in during her long illness
before stigmatization, an illness resulting from the dislo-
cation of her spinal cord, yet Resl's richly fitted interior
life would have won over her physical states, suppressing
the ego entirely and giving herself wholly to God. Professor Mager says: "Theresa Neumann is a strong character, in whom religion conquered the spiritual and moral
side of hysteria or at least prevented it from playing the
more important role."

The variety of Therese's ecstatic phenomena, wounds,
historical visions, the speaking of foreign languages, and
the gift of prophecy — these cannot all be explained by
hysteria. Those who do not presume to delve into the
mazes of psychology in its many phases may well ask, If
the ecstasies and visions of the Passion are caused by
Therese's devotion to her suffering Lord, why does she
also have visions which have nothing to do with Christ's
Passion? She has visions of Christ as a child, of Him in
an hour of triumph and glory, as on Mount Tabor; and
visions of events or personages in which she had no special
interest, may never have known or thought about.

Therese Neumann's ecstasies and the visions during
them have met the test of spiritual results. Contrary to
the moral disturbances caused by hysteria or other pathological conditions, her ecstasies have produced an ever
increasing love of God, a constant desire for perfection,
and an unfailing willingness to suffer for God and the
souls for whom He died. Farges, a writer on mysticism,
says that mystical phenomena are neither diseased nor

brought forth by illness. On the contrary, they react
beneficially on illnesses. St. Teresa of Ávila was greatly
strengthened, both physically and morally, by her ecstasies.
Therese of Konnersreuth, after the twelve-hour Friday
ecstasy with loss of blood, will recover completely in such
a short time that she is well again by Sunday. The state
of exalted rest grants her the supernatural refreshment
of which St. Teresa speaks. The great Spanish mystic
wrote that often the one who was sickly and full of pain
becomes healthy and even stronger, "for it is something
great that is given to the soul in rapture," and sometimes
God wishes to have the body rejoice, because it has been
obedient to the soul.

Other factors, too, the regularity of the ecstasies and
their relation to the liturgy, their exalted beauty even in
the midst of pain and blood; above all, the sublimity of
their themes and the nobility of the mystic's mimicry —
all these testify to their more than natural source.

The report that in Konnersreuth there lived a young
woman who neither ate nor drank, caused quite a com-
motion twenty years ago. As we know, there was a strict
two-week observation which established nothing to please
the skeptics but supported the contention of those who
believed Therese Neumann really lived without earthly
food or drink. Nothing has happened since then to shake
this conviction, to lessen the faith of so many in the
supernatural character of this and all the other Konnersreuth phenomena.

A psychiatrist's verdict on the Konnersreuth phenomena, more recent than Dr. Chideckel's, is that of Dr.
Hubert J. Urban, head of the psychiatric-neurological

clinic of Innsbruck University. His verdict is not given from afar nor does it follow upon a false report of Therese Neumann's death. It results from a visit to Konnersreuth in October, 1944, during which he was allowed to be present during an ecstasy of the Passion and to examine the stigmatist closely.

Of Resl's complete abstinence from food, Dr. Urban says: "This supernatural phenomenon is, of course, a negative thing and cannot be investigated during one brief visit. But the personality of Therese Neumann and the atmosphere in which she lives do not permit the slightest doubt to arise concerning the genuineness of her fasting." He notes that there are no *Ausscheidungen,* no excretions of any kind, as would be the case if nourishment were taken.

Dr. Urban sums up his observation by saying that the Konnersreuth phenomena are neither sickness nor deception; that the proved sudden cures cannot be explained naturally. He suggests an investigation by an international commission of experts, the membership of which would include differing viewpoints; a commission which would be prepared to accept the results, even if they served to prove the supernatural character of the phenomena. He closes his report with the opinion that nothing can give a clear picture of the amazing Konnersreuth phenomena excepting a visit to Therese Neumann's village and a close study of the stigmatist. And he is thankful that he has had this privilege, especially thankful as a man of medicine.[6]

One of the most recent observations on the Konners-

6 *Volksblatt,* Basel, Switzerland, March 26–28, 1947.

reuth phenomena appears in a German magazine, publication of which began since the end of the war. The author says that as a layman he does not wish to meddle in the quarrels of men of medicine, but he wishes to tell of an experience of his at the bedside of Therese Neumann, on Friday, July 8, 1927. The feet of the stigmatist were bare and, as she lay in ecstasy and shared in the hammering of the nails at Christ's crucifixion, her feet twitched with pain. "Soon a drop of blood which increased in size formed at one of the foot stigmata. It grew and grew in size until finally it dropped from the wound. Gravity would have commanded that the drop of blood flow downwards. But it didn't. It flowed almost directly upwards, toward the toes, as happened almost 2000 years ago on the cross of Christ!"

The writer continues: "There is on earth no power which can force a freely flowing drop to flow upwards, not even the world-witch hysteria. Later the pastor told me that this disregard of a law of nature was usual, and on the arms, too." He asks, who can thus command the laws of nature? "Surely none but He who made them."

At the close of his article this student of the Konnersreuth case says that the Church has, prudently, spoken no decisive word regarding the phenomena, and, of course, he has no least intention to anticipate her verdict. He is of the opinion that what happens in Konnersreuth is of itself of small importance so far as Therese Neumann is concerned. Only when her life has come to an end and lies open to the Church's decision, it may be that the miracles worked *on* her will weigh nothing or but little in comparison to miracles which may one day be worked *through* her. "What I have tried to give, free of all polemics, is a description to the objective truth of which I am ready to pledge myself. Perhaps it will seem to my readers it is amazing enough."[7]

[7] Aretin, Erwein Freiherr von, in *Berliner Hefte*, No. 4, Sept., 1940, pp. 264, 265.

CHAPTER 18: The World Watches

WHEN Therese Neumann's sight was restored to her on April 23, 1923, after more than four years of blindness, neighbors came to the Neumann house to congratulate *Schneiderixenresl*, the good-natured, kindhearted young woman whom everybody liked and respected, whose many afflictions had called forth the sympathy of the whole village. Resl's happy mother sent word to Godmother Forster in Waldsassen.

Gradually the good news of this and the succeeding cures spread, but as yet by word of mouth only or by an occasional letter. The news spread much more rapidly by means of the ubiquitous press, when it became known that Therese was stigmatized, had ecstasies and visions, and continued to live without eating or drinking. The Konnersreuth case became like a pebble dropped into the humdrum life of a sequestered village and thence spreading ripples of excitement in all directions. It spread across the near-by border between Bavaria and Czechoslovakia, to all parts of Germany and Western Europe, and across the seas to the Americas and to the East. The world began to watch.

Visitors came in constantly increasing numbers. They found what all of the villagers could have told them, that Resl had not been spoiled in the least by what had happened. She remained the peasant maid who preferred her country dialect to High German, and was interested in the daily life of her home and village, in flowers, animals, birds. They found that she had lost none of her native simplicity and mother wit, nor the straightforward outlook on life in which truth is sacred.

"I may have seen another person as far removed from any egotistical thoughts, but I have never seen one so remarkably free from all vanity," wrote Freiherr von Aretin. "She has in nowise stepped beyond the natural boundaries of her being. In her own estimation she is still the servant girl of 1918, and without the least desire to appear more than that. An old woman of the village lay dying, and without saying anything to anyone, but also without seeking to keep it a secret, Therese hobbled to the house of death so she might with tactful words solace the last moments of the old woman."[1]

Another observer called the stigmatist "beyond all doubt the most unassuming, the most upright and truthful child in the whole world." Still another stressed the fact that Resl is not in the least high strung, nervous, or neurotic; and that her piety is thoroughly wholesome. Because of her passionate devotion to truth, in regard to her ecstatic visions as to all other things, Therese is sensitive toward charges of unreliability. But her attitude to the personal charge of fraud is shown by her statement reported by Dr. Hollnsteiner: "Do you know, I like him

[1] Von Aretin, in *Berliner Hefte*, No. 4, Sept., 1946, pp. 264, 265.

who tells me in the morning that I am a fraud just as much as the one who tells me in the evening that I am a saint. I am sorry for both of them, because of their stupidity. The one is stupid because he believes such things can be 'invented'; the other because he doesn't seem to know that, while all of us hope to be saints some day, we are a long way from it as yet."

But the people of Konnersreuth knew and the visitors learned, if they came with understanding hearts and unbiased minds, that a tremendous change had come over Therese Neumann in the realm of the spirit. The visitors found one who had climbed the three high and perilous stairs which only those may ascend who respond when God offers them the extraordinary graces of mysticism, which graces do not mar but preserve and transfigure human nature.

There is abundant testimony in the words of those who saw Therese soon or some time after the news of Konnersreuth's wonders had spread abroad. "If we speak of Therese, she refers at once to 'the dear Saviour' and what He wills she wills, and naught else. He knows how to manage all things; He is 'so good,' and 'He can do all things.' " Again, "Her views are thoroughly sound and all her interests have as their ultimate object the Saviour whom she loves so much. . . . Her large blue eyes bespeak the peace of her soul; they are merry, not moody or melancholy. . . . She herself is convinced that what is happening to her is from above. But within her, strong and living, is the consciousness that this is not due to her own merits or powers, but only to the grace of God. Despite all the great things she has experienced, her humility cannot be disturbed in the least. . . . To be a child in the sight of God and willingly and gladly conform to His will, that is the whole of her wisdom." If it were not God's will, if only her preference were to be considered, she would rather not be a mystic, the center of so much attention. She said to a Jesuit in November, 1926: "As far as I am concerned, they can put me in jail or hang me on the church steeple, if only God's holy will is done!"

Johannes Mayrhofer, the author of a book on Konnersreuth, reported that Therese tried to hide the stigmata, and would like best of all to be let alone. "When a senseless person wrote that she ought to be put in a jail or reformatory, she expressed her opinion with perfect complacency, 'There I could speak with God, too, and I would be free from visitors!' But in childlike obedience to the command from above and the advice of her spiritual director, she submits calmly and with friendliness to the many burdensome visits."[2]

Antonie von Taenzl declared that nothing was so painful for Resl as to have the attention of so many drawn to her. "She has repeatedly told priests that she would gladly suffer all for God, if He would only take away the exceptional, that which attracts attention. She endures the 'sight-seers' and the many visitors with patience and submission to God's will. She does not wish to cut herself off from the public, if the sight of her suffering leads some to God and to a better mode of life."[3]

Thus the watching world saw or read about Therese Neumann in quiet moments of conversation, in her home,

[2] *Allgemeine Rundschau*, No. 29, July 17, 1926.
[3] *Beyrische Kirchenzeitung*, No. 47, Nov. 21, 1926.

where she did what work her condition allowed; or in the garden, whose flowers she delighted in and heaped upon the altars of the village church as an expression of her deep devotion. They saw or read about the other Therese, too, the sufferer of Konnersreuth, submerged in a sea of unutterable woe when she shared in her Redeemer's agony; in transports of joy when her visions were of the Christ Child, of Jesus in triumph, of the Blessed Virgin Mother or one of the saints; or enraptured in mystical ecstasy of union with Him whom her soul loves.

Next to the stigmatist, interest centered in the Rev. Joseph Naber, the pastor of the Church of St. Lawrence. This was inevitable, because of his position. He had been Therese's parish priest since her tenth year, her spiritual director, her friendly counselor throughout the long ordeal of her many sicknesses, throughout the amazing cures, and ever since the first stigmata and the first ecstasy.

One of the many who have written of Resl has stated that "On the bridge between the thousands of visitors and the solitary girl stands the tireless parish priest, constantly wrestling with himself as to which is his higher duty, to lead the people across the bridge or to prevent them from crossing it. It is a perpetual contest in his conscience, and it has deep roots. He himself has told me of it, in substance as follows: 'It is true, we are offended by the curiosity of the people and we should like best of all to admit no one at all. But do we know what God's intentions are in regard to Resl? It seems to me He wishes the people to learn something of the wonderful facts and events.'" Sometime later another quotes him as saying: "Resl has received a revelation that through her suffering many would be directed toward the other world, and so she must bear patiently what this brings with it. And neither do I wish to oppose it and offend against the will of God."

Father Naber has discharged his difficult task with a keen sense of duty toward Therese and the public and in strict accordance with the instructions of his superiors in the Church. And Resl, on her part, has followed faithfully and gladly the admonition of the voice to be guided by him in all that pertains to her spiritual life, the life which is to her so much more important than the things of earth.

Therese Neumann's family is, of course, of interest to all who are interested in her. Of her parents, Ferdinand and Anna Neumann, and of her nine brothers and sisters, may be said what was said of their Resl, all that has happened has not spoiled them. Like their daughter and sister they believe that the phenomena are of God, and so reverence is added to the affection with which they surrounded her when she was for years a bedridden invalid in their humble home. They did not welcome, but it would never have occurred to them to oppose, the terrible, mysterious manifestations of a more than natural power. And Therese's healing meant new worries for them, a heavy burden. They disliked as intensely as Resl, to have their home invaded by throngs, to be pestered to such an extent at times that Herr Neumann's work as tailor and farmer was seriously hampered, as also the work of Frau Neumann. It hurt them to see their daughter the cynosure of so many eyes, not all of them friendly and reverent; to have her the center of controversy. The father consented to have Resl watched in their home for fifteen days, to establish the fact of her complete abstinence from nourishment, but Herr Neumann would not allow her to be taken to a "neutral" clinic, least of all after he had heard of the brutal attitude of some of the doctors, who spoke of the "Catholic" injections they would give Resl once they had her in their power.

One thing stands out above all else in regard to the family of Therese Neumann: they never capitalized in the least degree the extraordinary events which made Konnersreuth known throughout the world. A visitor in August, 1927, wrote of the "humble, one-story home, in the attic of which a little room had been built for the stigmatist. The house had not been large enough, and the influx of visitors made repairs urgent, so Herr Neumann enlarged and improved it a bit with funds borrowed from his sister, a credit union, and the parish. But the sum was not sufficient, so all the members of the family, including Therese, took part in the building work."

Another said: "Business enterprises could have been found that would have rebuilt the Neumann house into a theater. Millions would have been paid if Theresa in her suffering condition would have been filmed and been shown in the motion-picture houses of Europe."[4] Herr Neumann rejected all offers, declares Archbishop Teodorowicz. The family refuses to take advantage in any way of the phenomena. The Neumanns care nothing for the favor of those who come to Konnersreuth, "be they who they may." A member of a former ruling family knocked in vain at the door: he had no proper admission card. A lady of high rank was offended because she was addressed

[4] From a sermon by Cardinal Faulhaber of Munich, quoted in *Zeitrufe–Gottesrufe*, 1932, p. 130.

as *"du."* No one cared. No matter how humble or how eminent persons were, they were admitted, providing they had the necessary permits demanded by the Regensburg diocesan authorities and were in no way objectionable to Herr Neumann or to Therese.

Father McHugh, whose letter on Konnersreuth has been quoted, says: "The complete lack of commercialism of the astounding events surrounding Theresa is most satisfying. Without doubt, millions could have been made in the past nineteen years from the hundreds of thousands of visitors, but there is not even a trace of money visible. The Neumanns still live in the modest Bavarian cottage which would sell in the States, in normal times, at between $1,500 and $2,000."[5]

Nor do the people of Konnersreuth seek to commercialize the presence of the stigmatist woman in their midst. "Many of the visitors remain a number of days. Not only do the people accept no remuneration beyond their actual expenses, but they often accommodate people, particularly priests, without accepting anything at all. Father Naber especially gives without any recompense whatever his time and his great patience; more than one of those whose words have been written down in this book was his guest for days, and never was there the least indication of a desire for gain. And Therese's parents, too, refuse absolutely to accept any donations."[6] The whole atmosphere of Therese's village is a tribute to its Catholic faith, to the influence of its pastor and of its native daughter who, without having wished it, made Konnersreuth one of the

[5] From mimeographed letter dated Jan. 30, 1945.
[6] Von Lama, *Therese Neumann*, p. 199.

widest-known, most written-about, talked-about places in
the world.

Among the thousands upon thousands of visitors to
Konnersreuth since 1926 have been members of the
Catholic hierarchy from all parts of the world, including
Brazil, India, Canada, Africa; many priests, monks and
friars, writers, physicians, representatives of the sciences,
— men and women of almost all walks in life. And since
the end of World War II, soldiers of the American and
other armies stationed in or near Germany have visited
Therese. Cardinal Faulhaber saw the stigmatist on August
24, 1928, offered up Mass in her room and gave her Holy
Communion. He, like other Konnersreuth visitors, was
to be persecuted later by the Nazi tyrants. On October 20,
1928, Bishop Buchberger of Regensburg had an audience
with Pope Pius XI and gave His Holiness a special report
on the phenomena. Earlier in the year, on March 23, and
again in April, there came to Konnersreuth Father Agos-
tino Gemelli, O.F.M., rector of the Catholic University
of Milan, a specialist in the fields of medicine and psy-
chiatry, "who had once fought in the ranks of Socialism."
After his report to the Holy Father, Pius XI on May 3,
1928, sent his blessing to Therese Neumann and Father
Naber.

Among the visitors have been an official of the Lutheran
State church of Sweden and other Protestants; officers of
the Russian Black Sea fleet; also Jews and adherents of
various pseudo-scientific, antisupernatural philosophies;
and at least one actress, the American Lilian Gish. In
Numbers 40, 41, and 42, of October, 1929, the *Konners-
reuther Sonntagsblatt* said that the actress arrived in the

village on Wednesday, September 5, 1928. Her traveling companion, a young woman from Salzburg, said that Miss Gish's mother was critically ill and the intercession of the stigmatist in her behalf was the purpose of the actress's visit. It had been previously reported that Max Reinhardt, the noted impressario, intended to produce a motion picture for which Hugo von Hofmannsthal's manuscript was to be based on Therese of Konnersreuth with Lilian Gish in the title role. Did the scheme come to naught because of Miss Gish's interview with the stigmatist and presence at a Passion ecstasy?

It is twenty years, now, that the world has been watching Konnersreuth. It has watched with belief, reverence, sympathy, and supplication; or with unbelief, wavering interest, and scoffing. Even animosity has been shown. But the scrutiny has been borne with honor by the village, by the Neumann family, Father Naber and the villagers; and by Therese, serenely enduring, humbly rising by God's will to spiritual heights dizzying to ordinary men and women. In a Lenten sermon in 1931, Cardinal Faulhaber said: "There are sacrificial souls within and without the cloister which are like unto altar candles of sacrifice, burning slowly out of love for the Redeemer. And above such beds of pain there hovers a glow of transfiguration."

Von Lama wrote: "This glow of transfiguration above the bed of Therese Neumann's suffering has been seen by many. Its perception depends upon the personal disposition of the visitor; perhaps, also, upon the will of God." He stated that Resl's *Freitagsleiden* were the origin and impetus to conversions, both of lapsed Catholics returning to the practice of their religion, and of non-Catholics entering the Fold. There was the university lecturer from Vienna who said to Father Naber: *"Herr Pfarrer,* thank Resl for me!" and to the stigmatist, "Resl, I thank you, you have given me back my faith!" Among the converts from Protestantism have been Counselor Schondorf; Dr. Becker, who had come to regard the Saviour as no more than one of the great initiated ones, no higher than the so-called Mahatmas; and the thirty-second degree Mason who visited Konnersreuth in 1928 and was received into the Church after returning to the United States, according to the report of a priest in Madison, Wisconsin. The converts from Judaism have included Dr. Karpeles of Vienna and Bruno Rothschild, who became a priest.

From the bed to which she is so often chained by pain, from the humble home in a Bavarian village, Resl of Konnersreuth has continued to practice her vocation, has carried on her apostolate; has, not by herself but through the divine Originator of the phenomena, turned the minds and hearts of men upwards. She has done this in such a way as to merit and gain the reverent admiration of all who have observed her, and have studied the phenomena with love of the truth uppermost in their minds. Two of the many, deserving to be called Knights of Konnersreuth, were Friedrich Ritter von Lama and Dr. Fritz Gerlich. Love of the truth led them to study and then to defend the Konnersreuth happenings against prejudices and false charges, and love of the truth led them to death at the hands of the Nazis, whose power was based on lies.

Friedrich von Lama, a native of Salzburg, Austria, grew up in Bavaria. He was associated with the publishing firm of Pustet in Regensburg and was widely known for his volumes on Therese Neumann. He was also the author of other books, including a biography of Pope Pius XI.

Dr. Gerlich was the non-Catholic editor of the Liberal *Münchener Neueste Nachrichten* when he became aware of demands for official interference at Konnersreuth. "It seemed for a time that the assertions of scientific and other interests would be sufficient to cause the violation of the constitutional rights and in particular the personal freedom of this girl of unblemished character, and to make her the defenseless object of more or less justified investigations and experiments." Against this his sense of justice rebelled. In 1927 he made the first of his visits to Therese Neumann's village. He studied the phenomena with scientific thoroughness and complete objectivity. The result was that he abjured the Calvinistic errors in which he had been reared, met the demands of the Church regarding a marriage matter, and became a Catholic. Resl was his godmother when he was baptized conditionally on September 29, 1931, and received Holy Communion for the first time in the Capuchin church at Eichstätt. During the little feast which followed, the stigmatist was rapt in a vision and saw the Little Flower, who through Therese wished to congratulate the convert.

Ritter von Lama told what happened to Dr. Gerlich, who loved truth and the rights of man. When the Hitler gangsters rose to power in March, 1933, Fritz Gerlich was one of the first to be arrested. "Until June 30, 1934, he was a prisoner. On that day he was called from his cell and without any charge in court ever having been brought against him, he was taken out and shot." It took courage for Von Lama to write this, for the executioners of Gerlich had become steadily more and more powerful and brutal.

Perhaps the Nazis took note of what Ritter von Lama had written about Dr. Gerlich, and of course they knew him as an unalterable opponent of their cruel and neo-pagan program. After a long silence, word came from his widow, Christa von Lama, that her husband had been murdered by the Gestapo on February 6, 1944. A National Catholic Welfare Conference News Service report, dated Munich, March 17, 1947, says that Von Lama went to the gallows in Stadelheim prison in February, 1944, "carrying a rosary around his neck." He had been sentenced to death by a Gestapo court, after having been imprisoned a number of times. His only son, Franz, a journalist in Vienna, died at Dachau.

May we not believe that Resl of Konnersreuth knew how to help these Knights of Konnersreuth when they faced death?